Spirit
of
Truth

'In a topic usually known more for its disagreements, Jackman steers a sure-footed course through the main lines of thought about the Holy Spirit. Every Christian should be a theologian of the Holy Spirit and this book will greatly help us in this goal. It carries us along, with skillful and pastoral insight, to a greater appreciation for the third Person of the Trinity.'

Derek W. H. Thomas

John E. Richards Professor of Systematic and Practical Theology,
Reformed Theological Seminary, Jackson, Mississippi
Minister of Teaching, First Presbyterian Church, Jackson
Editorial Director, Alliance of Confessing Evangelicals

Spirit
of
Truth

*Unlocking the Bible's Teaching
on the Holy Spirit*

David Jackman

CHRISTIAN
FOCUS

David Jackman is the President of the Proclamation Trust & Director of the Cornhill Training Course, London. Their aim is to effectively communicate the gospel, especially through preaching. David's other titles include *Teaching Matthew: Unlocking the Gospel of Matthew for the Expositor* (ISBN 978-1-84550-877-8) and *Teaching the Christian Hope: Unlocking Biblical Eschatology for the Expositor* (ISBN 978-1-84550-518-0)

Copyright © Proclamation Trust Media 2006

ISBN 1-84550-057-1
ISBN 978-1-84550-057-3

10 9 8 7 6 5 4 3 2 1

Published in 2006
Reprinted 2007
by
Christian Focus Publications,
Geanies House, Fearn,
Ross-shire, IV20 1TW, Scotland, Great Britain
with
Proclamation Trust Media,
Willcox House, 140-148 Borough High Street,
London, SE1 1LB, England, Great Britain.
www.proctrust.org.uk

www.christianfocus.com

Cover design by Moose77.com

Printed and bound by
Nørhaven Paperback A/S, Denmark

CONTENTS

FOREWORD

It is a great pleasure and privilege to have been asked by Christian Focus Publications to prepare this second and considerably revised version of *Spirit of Truth* for publication. The book first appeared in 1993 as a series of simple, straightforward expositions of key Biblical passages about the person and work of the Holy Spirit. All of its chapters began as preached material, several at the Keswick Convention and some others at Above Bar Church in Southampton, where I was the senior minister from 1980 to 1991. The aim was to provide an overview of the Bible's teaching in a format which could be used equally for personal or for group study. The basic structure of the book remains the same in this second edition. However, as the times have changed and fresh issues have been raised, I have added to many of the chapters some further explanation and detail, which I hope will help to clarify some more urgent contemporary causes of debate or confusion.

In the foreword to the first edition, I asked the questions, "So, why yet another book about the Holy Spirit? Haven't we already enough to fill a library?" The same could be said today with even greater justification, but I think my answers then remain remarkably relevant now and so I would like to rehearse them, briefly.

Firstly, in all the debate about the charismatic movement over the past thirty years, much of the written material has been produced specifically to develop, or answer, rather specific and detailed arguments about particular experiences or phenomena. There is a danger in that; namely that this whole area of Christian thought and experience is expected to generate more heat than light. For many Christians the great and glorious Biblical truths about the Holy Spirit have been lost in the cross-fire of argument and counter-argument, so that the whole subject has become a ground of contention and dispute, rather than of enlightenment and joy. There is a place, I believe, for a simple restatement of the great doctrines of the Spirit's person and work for a new generation of Christians, many of whom have been forced to adopt positions and take sides in arguments, perhaps without fully realizing the foundation principles on which such discussions are based.

Secondly, my method is simply to allow the Bible to speak for itself. There is no special pleading here for a particular view or position, other than that which is clearly taught in Scripture. I have often said, when teaching the Bible, "Don't believe this because I say it. Only believe it if you are convinced the Bible is saying it". My main concern therefore has been to write each chapter as an exposition of a Bible passage, because I believe that one of the greatest needs in the universal church today is to learn to listen carefully to Scripture and therefore this method runs through all my teaching. The text of the passage has been printed at the start of each chapter, so that the material can still be studied even if a Bible is not to hand. Although all the material has been re-worked, I hope and pray that something of the preacher's urgency will also be communicated through these pages.

Thirdly, in an age still dedicated to the quest for spiritual experience, we need to reassert the authority of the Bible as the only arbiter of which experiences come from God, and which do not. Spiritual reality is not to be judged by the intensity of our emotion, but by the revelation of God's will. We can only recognise any experience to be of God if we know what God

Foreword

is like and how he relates to us, and for that we are entirely dependent on the Word of God. Christianity is an experiential religion, but its experience is produced by the Word which God has spoken and continues to speak.

There is a special appropriateness in this, for it is the Holy Spirit who inspired the Word and it is still his great tool in the work of bringing people to Christ and building them up in the faith. It is still true that a great deal of our current confusion is caused by a false polarization of the Word and the Spirit. It is false because it is untrue to both. Yet how many Christians have opted in one direction or the other, as though such a "choice" was perfectly legitimate? On the one side, there is the caricature of the 'Word' Christians – cerebral, logical, all head and no heart. Their concern is with doctrine, truth and orthodoxy. On the other side, equally victims of caricature, are the 'Spirit' Christians – emotional, intuitive, warm, plenty of heart but no head. Their concern is with experience, love and excitement. Surely we cannot be content with these wooden travesties of real Christian faith and love any longer! There can be no division between Word and Spirit, truth and love, doctrine and experience, mind and heart. They all belong together, in New Testament Christianity, always. My hope and prayer is that in some small way these studies may help a new generation to repent where we have been guilty of "putting asunder" what God has joined together, and prevent us from repeating the mistakes of the past in the future.

I am very grateful to several friends and colleagues who have encouraged me to re-issue the book, in the light of something of a perceived gap in the market for basic and straightforward expository material at this level. I am equally grateful to the Trustees of the Proclamation Trust for their support and to Nancy Olsen for her skilful expertise and enthusiastic commitment to preparing the manuscript for publication. Special thanks are due to Pete Nicholas, currently working with me as my study assistant, who re-read the original manuscript and who raised penetrating questions and made invaluable suggestions about how the material might relate more effectively to issues within the contemporary debate. His work provided a very valuable stimulus to my thinking. Finally, I want to thank my wife, Heather, for her help and support, as always over the thirty-five years of our marriage, in "getting the job done", which is one way of translating the word "dunamis" – the power of the Spirit of Truth. Glory be to God!

London
September 2005

1.
IDENTIFYING THE SPIRIT'S ROLE

We begin with a bedrock principle, taught throughout the Scriptures, that the Holy Spirit is the divine third person of the Holy Trinity. Every orthodox Christian would of course readily agree to this central proposition, but many of us fail to draw out its implications. One is that the Spirit must never be thought of as a vague influence or divine essence. He is infinite, yet he is always personal, because he is God. The Holy Spirit is just as much God as the Lord Jesus is, though without a human body, of course. But his invisibility and lack of bodily form in no way diminish his deity. So we must never allow ourselves to be trapped into using the impersonal pronoun "it" to describe the Spirit or his work. He is for ever God, utterly divine.

WHO THE SPIRIT IS

There are several clear strands of Biblical evidence which lead us to this conclusion. The first mention of the Spirit in Scripture is in Genesis 1:2, where he is depicted as "hovering over the waters", clearly identified as the divine agent in creation. The Hebrew word translated "Spirit" is "ruach", which means breath or wind, and this characteristic of the Spirit develops in two major directions. Our English word "spirit" is derived from the Latin "spiro" – I breathe. Sometimes the breath of God is revealed and experienced as mighty power, in a rushing wind, as on the day of Pentecost. As Leon Morris once commented, "After all, what is a wind, but a lot of breath in a hurry?" Certainly, there is no doubt about the Spirit's power to bring created order out of formless chaos, and we shall return to that concept often when we see the key New Testament term "dunamis", to describe his ability to accomplish his will. This aspect reminds us that the Spirit is an irresistible gale, to which we must trim our sails if we are to experience God's dynamic ability in Christian life and service.

But the "ruach" theme also develops into the idea of the inspiration of the Word of God, as when Paul reminds Timothy in 2 Timothy 3:16 that "all Scripture is God-breathed", which is a very literal translation. What we call "inspiration" is actually God breathing out the thoughts of His mind in the words of revelation, and this is necessarily the activity of the divine Spirit, for "no one knows the thoughts of God except the Spirit of God" (1 Cor. 2:11). Not surprisingly then, going back to Genesis 1, we find that the third verse states, "And God said, 'Let there be light' and there was light". This links together the divine word and the divine power in the creative work of the Holy Spirit. It is a theme which the psalmists loved to repeat and develop, as they also linked the power of God inextricably to the Word of God. "By the word of the Lord were the heavens made, their starry host by the breath of his mouth" (Ps. 33:6). "When you send your Spirit, they are created, and you renew the face of the earth" (Ps. 104:30).

If the Spirit's role is creative in the physical universe, it comes as no surprise to learn that in the spiritual realm his work is to regenerate sinful men and women, to bring about the new birth. In the words of Jesus, "Unless a man is born of water and the Spirit, he cannot enter the kingdom of God. Flesh gives birth to flesh, but the Spirit gives birth to spirit"

(John 3:5-6). Paul makes the same point about the Spirit's role as the author and giver of eternal life in Romans 8:11. "He who raised Christ from the dead will also give life to your mortal bodies through his spirit, who lives in you."

There is a sense, then, in which Scripture establishes the deity of the Spirit solely by reference to his characteristic activity. Only God could do these things! But then his deity is spelt out more specifically in a variety of other ways. "Where can I go from your Spirit? Where can I flee from your presence?" asks the Psalmist, and proceeds to expound the fact that the Spirit of the Lord is everywhere. "If I go up to the heavens, you are there; if I make my bed in the depths, you are there" (Psalm 139:7ff). Omnipresence is a uniquely divine characteristic, as is omnipotence. It is this latter characteristic to which Isaiah draws attention, in a series of rhetorical questions. "Who has understood the Spirit of the LORD, or instructed him as his counsellor? Whom did the LORD consult to enlighten him, and who taught him the right way? Who was it that taught him knowledge or showed him the path of understanding?" (Isa. 40:13-14). The point he is making is that the Spirit is totally self sufficient because he is divine.

The very fact that his characteristic description is as the holy Spirit (Ps. 51:11) also affirms his deity, for holiness is not so much an attribute or quality of God, as the Biblical description of his very essence and being. He is God's Spirit (1 Cor. 3:16), and therefore the Spirit of glory (1 Peter 4:14), another of God's unique attributes. To lie to the Holy Spirit is therefore to lie to God, as Peter made explicit to Ananias in Acts 5:3-4. Implicit also in all these passages is the personality of the Spirit. He is the third person of the Trinity and as such he can be grieved (Eph. 4:30) or quenched (1 Thess. 5:19). But he is also pro-active, in all sorts of ways which are characteristic only of a person. An examination of the verb, of which the Holy Spirit is the subject, across the whole Bible, soon indicates that no mere "influence" or "impersonal power" could be spoken about in these terms. All of the communication statements (he speaks, commands, testifies) as well as other activities, such as creation, giving life to the dead and interceding for God's people presuppose personality. They are not just personification, which is a literary device used sparingly in Scripture, but expressions of personhood.

The difficulty has centred historically on the impression that the term "spirit" is less personal than either "Father" or "Son". Moreover, the invisibility and omnipresence of the Spirit make it harder for us to comprehend his person and work compared with the visible bodily revelation of the Son, in his incarnation. Sometimes it is argued that the Greek word for spirit, "pneuma", is neuter and therefore not personal. But against that stands the fact that the masculine pronoun is used about him (not "it") during Jesus' upper room teaching (eg John 14:16). Moreover, Jesus designates the Spirit as the "paraclete" (John 14:26, 15:26, 16:7) which is a personal term, since he will be "another comforter" sent to be a replacement for the person of the Lord Jesus who is returning to the Father. The root meaning of "parakletos" must be the one who fulfils the activity of coming alongside to strengthen and help, a role which can only make sense if it is operated by a living person. Indeed to speak, as the New Testament consistently does, of the presence or power of the Holy Spirit would be quite meaningless if some impersonal abstract influence was in view.

In summary, the full deity and personhood of the Holy Spirit is established in two classic New Testament verses. The first is usually described as the Great Commission, where the Lord Jesus sends his disciples into the world to make disciples and to baptise them in the Trinitarian name of the Father, Son and Holy Spirit (Matt. 28:19). The other is the equally significant formulation of "the grace" given by Paul at the end of 2 Corinthians. "May the grace of the Lord Jesus Christ, and the love of God, and the fellowship of the Holy Spirit be with you all" (2 Cor. 13:14). The Nicene Creed is thoroughly

Biblical, then, when it affirms of the Holy Spirit that he is "the Lord, the life-giver, who proceeds from the Father, who with the Father and the Son is together worshipped and together glorified". Such Biblical clarity will stop us from divorcing the power from the person, or the gifts from the giver. It should deter us from seeking spiritual experiences for their own sake and make us hungry for more of God himself.

What The Spirit Does

Paul's first letter to the Corinthians is largely concerned with discerning true spiritual realities from the false and spurious counterfeits with which the church was becoming dazzled and obsessed. A key verse in his argument is 1 Corinthians 12:3, "No-one can say, 'Jesus is Lord', except by the Holy Spirit." He is not thinking of merely mouthing the words, of course, but of a meaningful personal confession of belief, which constituted the earliest Christian creed. This opens up to us the major activities of the Spirit, on which the New Testament focuses.

The Spirit's work is to reveal the true nature of Christ and to bring men and women to worship him through faith and obedience. In order to do this, he inspired the authors of Scripture to write the testimony which he revealed to them. Not only is the Spirit active in inspiration, but also in illumination as the Scriptures are read and understood. He brings understanding and conviction to our minds and hearts, granting us repentance towards God and the gift of new life through faith in the Lord Jesus. It is the same Spirit who works in each of us Christians to restore the defaced image of God in us, through the process we call sanctification. We become more like the Lord Jesus in our character and behaviour, only by the Spirit's power. Because he constitutes the church, the company of true believers who are therefore Christ's body on earth, he also rules in that new community, cultivating his fruit, dispersing his gifts and energising his witness. Without the Spirit's ministry there would be no Bible, no gospel, no new birth, no progress in holiness, no unity among believers. No-one would know Jesus as Lord were it not for the work of the Holy Spirit. Let's explore what this means in a little more detail.

The Spirit's great work is to reveal God to mankind. In this the whole Trinity is of course involved because "the Father sent the Son to be the Saviour of the world" (1 John 4:14). At the heart of the gospel lies the revelation that God is love, that he longs to bring us sinful men and women back into a living personal relationship with himself in spite of our sin and his righteousness, and that he has therefore intervened in our history by coming personally into this world as our redeemer. "When the time had fully come, God sent his Son, born of a woman, born under law, to redeem those under law, that we might receive the full right of sons" (Gal. 4:4-5). All this is objective historical fact. A truly human baby was really born at Bethlehem. He really lived and really died and really rose again. It happened! But how would we ever have known or how could we ever be sure, if these events had not been recorded for us and for all generations in the Scriptures? That is the Spirit's work.

He did it in Old Testament times by coming upon God's servants, the prophets, to inspire them to prophesy about Jesus. Peter has some key verses, which make this very plain. "The prophets, who spoke of the grace that was to come to you, searched intently and with the greatest care, trying to find out the time and circumstances to which the Spirit of Christ in them was pointing when he predicted the sufferings of Christ and the glories that would follow." (1 Peter 1:10-11). It was not only the Old Testament prophets who were dependent on the Holy Spirit, but the New Testament gospel preachers too. The apostolic ministry was a ministry of the Spirit. So, Peter continues to write about these open secrets "that have now been told you by those who have preached the gospel to you by the Holy Spirit sent from heaven" (v. 12). The truth is revealed only by the Spirit and only through God's word.

Listen to Peter again. "You must understand that no prophecy of Scripture came about by the prophet's own interpretation. For prophecy never had its origin in the will of man, but men spoke from God as they were carried along by the Holy Spirit" (2 Peter 1:20-21). Even before Pentecost, Peter had been fully aware that "the Scripture had to be fulfilled which the Holy Spirit spoke long ago..." (Acts 1:16). What Scripture says, God, the Holy Spirit, says, and whatever God says will happen. That is why we can have such confidence in the written word of God. It is the great gift of the Holy Spirit, to the church and to the world.

Speaking of the apostolic testimony, which witnessed the events of the life, death and resurrection of the Lord Jesus, confirming the words of the Old Testament prophets, Peter put both together and identified the Scriptures as the only reliable source of light to the Christian. "We have the word of the prophets made more certain, and you will do well to pay attention to it, as to a light shining in a dark place, until the day dawns and the morning star rises in your hearts" (2 Peter 1:19). Clearly, Peter is speaking about the last day, the day of Christ, when the Lord Jesus will be revealed at the end of time. He will come again to the world on that day in the full majesty of his hidden glory, to wind up human history and to bring in the fulness of his Kingdom. That is the far horizon to which all Christian believers look forward, when "we shall be like him, for we shall see him as he is" (1 John 3:2). But that day has not yet come, so the illumination is not yet internal. Until that day dawns, the light will be outside of ourselves, to be found in the written revelation. "Your word is a lamp to my feet and a light for my path" (Ps. 119:105).

But equally wonderful is the fact that the Spirit who originated the Word is also its great interpreter. "We speak of God's secret wisdom ... but God has revealed it to us by his Spirit" (1 Cor. 2:7-10). That wisdom is of course the Lord Jesus Christ himself (1 Cor. 1:30, Col. 2:3) and it is the great delight of the Spirit to testify to Christ and to open our spiritual eyes to see who he really is, in all his glory and grace. In Scripture then, not only do we have a divinely-inspired record of the events by which God has revealed himself, but also the divinely-given meaning of those events. The history together with the explanation constitute the Biblical revelation. Every believer has the privilege of the illumination of the Spirit in his or her life, but the Word of God is the divinely appointed channel through which the truth comes.

So we do have the indwelling Spirit to interpret and apply that word to all the changing scenes and situations of our lives. "The Spirit himself testifies with our spirit that we are God's children" (Rom. 8:16). He does this not by some warm subjective emotion, but by applying the clear testimony of the objective Word of God. "Because you are sons, God sent the Spirit of his Son into our hearts, the Spirit who calls out, Abba, Father." (Gal. 4:6). This is what Jesus meant when he promised that the counsellor whom he would send to his believing people from the Father would testify about Christ (John 15:26), "by taking from what is mine and making it known to you" (John 16:14). The Biblical picture is that Christ is our representative, in the presence of the Father, pleading the merits of his death and obtaining access for us into the holiest of all. He is our advocate, our great high priest who represents us in heaven. But in our hearts, the Holy Spirit is Christ's representative, making him real and precious to us. So Jesus promised, "I will ask the Father and he will give you another Counsellor to be with you for ever – the Spirit of truth" (John 14:16-17). This describes the Spirit's ministry, revealing Jesus in the Word of truth and so strengthening his people in their knowledge, love and obedience. He comes alongside to help us to apply the truth to our own situations and particular needs, as we reverently ask him to work in our minds, hearts and wills. And his activity is always Word-centred, because his work is always Christ-honouring. This is why Paul identifies the great offensive weapon which God has given us in our fight against the world, the flesh and the devil as "the sword of the Spirit, which is the Word of God" (Eph. 6:17).

HOW THE SPIRIT OPERATES

All this means that if we are to win in the battle, to grow in holiness and effective Christian living, we must know and use our Bibles. The Spirit has provided the sword. He trains us in its use. He gives us the strength to wield it. We are right to recognise that we are totally dependent upon the Holy Spirit, but the logical deduction is that we must therefore give ourselves to being diligent students of Scripture, and sadly that has become a comparatively rare priority among Christians today. We would prefer an instant "hot-line" from heaven. It's more culturally acceptable to us and saves a lot of time and trouble. Who wants to study a book, if there is an intuitive awareness of God's will open to us? The first can sound very "cerebral" and "rational", if not a little outdated. But that would be to ignore the greatest resource that God has given us. The teaching of the Bible is the plumb-line by which all claims to divine guidance, all new ideas, all intuitions must be tested. Its single, divine authorship means that Scripture has an inner harmony, without any contradictions.

There is a great deal of discussion and disagreement among Christians today about how God may, or may not, be speaking. "How do we discover his 'now' word?" is hotly debated. Some have described the Bible as a record of what God said yesterday, which needs to be augmented, if not replaced, by the words of contemporary prophets who will tell us what he is saying today. But what God said, he still says. His Word is eternal. Indeed, any contemporary claims to have a "word from the Lord" must be tested against the authoritative Word already given in Scripture. If they are in opposition to the Scripture, they are to be rejected. Such a simple test would have prevented hundreds of sincere people from being deluded by cultic leaders with powerful personalities. And if there is no Scriptural reference by which a prophecy can be tested, as for example when a prediction is made about future revival at a specific date, then the Old Testament test, that a true prophet speaks truth, has to be applied. "If what a prophet proclaims in the name of the Lord does not take place or come true, that is a message the Lord has not spoken. That prophet has spoken presumptuously" (Deut. 18:22). It is sobering to remember that false prophecy was punished by death in those days. The speaker could not simply say, "I got it wrong that time"!

This does not mean, however, that our individual, or even corporate, understanding of Scripture is infallible, particularly if we have taken little time to understand the Word in its own context. But we do need to recover the Reformers' confidence in what they called the "perspicuity" of Scripture, by which they meant that its message was predominantly clear and plain to the ordinary believer. The humble Christian, who depends upon the same Spirit who inspired the Word to interpret it, will not be disappointed or led astray. After all, God gave his Word to be our light, so he will not frustrate his own purposes. "If you then, though you are evil, know how to give good gifts to your children, how much more will your Father in heaven give good gifts to those who ask him!" (Matt. 7:11).

We have already noted the Holy Spirit's role as the creator and sustainer of life, but he is especially at work in the world, in a wider sense, in the lives of individual men and women. His mission is always to be the executive of the divine will within the world. As the crowning fulfilment of that great plan, there is the desire of the loving heart of God to draw out for himself a people who will be his own, and with whom he will dwell for ever – "a great multitude that no-one could count, from every nation, tribe, people and language" (Rev. 7:9). So the Holy Spirit's great work is to bring sinners to the Saviour and then to mature Christians in their faith, forming in them the likeness of Christ, the renewed image of God, so as to prepare them for heaven. That process must begin with the new birth, but the continual renewing work of the Spirit is the essence of Christian experience throughout our lives in this world.

We shall explore the Spirit's work in the world in more detail later, but here we need to note Jesus' comment that it will be a work of conviction – "of guilt in regard to sin and righteousness and judgment: in regard to sin, because men do not believe in me; in regard to righteousness, because I am going to the Father, where you can see me no longer; and in regard to judgment, because the prince of the world now stands condemned" (John 16:8-11). The sin of unbelief lies at the root of all our other sins. It is because we do not believe God's Word that we disobey it. It is because we do not believe that God has our best interests at heart that we will not allow him truly to be God in our lives. To be convicted of our unbelieving state by the Holy Spirit is the beginning of the gift of faith. This leads on to a recognition of the personal righteousness of the invisible Lord Jesus, confirmed by the Father through his resurrection and ascension. He is right and I am wrong. Then my eyes are opened to realise that Satan has already been overthrown by the cross and resurrection of the Lord Jesus and is under sentence of condemnation. Each of these supernatural realities is first brought to our attention by the Holy Spirit, who then burns them into our hearts and minds as we respond to his gracious teaching.

All this is underlining the fact that no-one can become a Christian without the work of the Holy Spirit in their life. He awakens our conscience and leads us to repent. He calls us to Christ, by revealing the truth of who Jesus is to our minds and applying it to our wills. He imparts his gift of saving faith, as we accept the forgiveness which Christ bought with his blood shed on the cross and as we become united to him both in his death and in his risen life. To be a Christian, therefore, is to receive the life of God within the innermost personality, or to be indwelt by the Holy Spirit. This is the obvious positive corollary of Paul's statement in Romans 8:9, "If anyone does not have the Spirit of Christ he does not belong to Christ." As the Spirit is the source of spiritual life within us, so he is the dynamic by which we are being made more like the Lord Jesus "being transformed into his likeness with ever increasing glory, which comes from the Lord, who is the Spirit" (2 Cor. 3:18). He produces his fruit in Christ-like character and enables us to mature as Christian disciples. He is our ability in prayer (Rom. 1:26), our guide and strength (Gal. 5:16,25) in the issues of life. He is the divine enabling by which we have everything we need to live a godly life in this world (2 Peter 1:3). His is the power which shields us from the world, the flesh and the devil, keeps us persevering in faith and obedience and who eventually will secure our safe arrival in our Father's heavenly home (1 Peter 1:3-5).

One further aspect of the Spirit's work is his rule within the church. Much of what has been said would perhaps appear excessively individualistic to the apostolic generation of believers. It is a tendency of our culture to be overly self-centred and to stress individual fulfilment at the price of corporate fellowship. But the Spirit, who indwells each Christian, also unites us all as members of the one body of Christ on earth. It is he who imparts the gifts of God's grace to the church, for the common good of all (1 Cor. 12:4-7). In his sovereignty, he decides which gifts shall be given to which individuals, but always with the aim of building up the whole (1 Cor. 12:11).

Yet underneath this God-given diversity of gifts and talents lies the foundational unity, which is the product of each member's individual dependence upon the Spirit's enabling. For Paul, this is "the unity of the Spirit", given in the gospel, but which we have to "make every effort to keep…in the bond of peace". There is one body just because there is one Spirit, animating every member (Eph 4:3-4). The commonality between us, whatever our background, gifts or experience, is the energising power of the Holy Spirit, the Lord, the giver of life. This explains why destruction of real unity is such a serious offence and why it can only be contemplated when fundamental doctrines of the faith are under attack or being denied. Otherwise it is an attack on the character of God himself, whose three persons are for ever one, in the unity of indestructible love, which is the very God-ness of God (1 John 4:8).

One outworking of this is the recognition that when God's people are responsive to the Spirit, this will be productive of unity, not division. Disintegration and disharmony are always indicative of sinful rebellion, usually based on individual pride. When those who claim unusual experiences of the Spirit proceed to impose their views upon congregations or individual believers in critical, unloving and divisive ways, a large question mark hangs over such claims. Too often churches have been divided and even ruined by aggressive and arrogant behaviour, in the name of some new understanding or experience of the Spirit. But his true mark is to unite God's people in the love which is his greatest gift and chief fruit. Do not accept inauthentic substitutes!

The Holy Spirit is also the enabling power behind the witness of the church in the world. He himself is the ability given to Christ's believing people, for the completion of the great commission to world evangelisation (Acts 1:8). We are completely dependent on his work for all spiritual progress. What Jesus said of himself to his disciples during his earthly ministry is as true now of the Spirit, the "other" Jesus, "apart from me, you can do nothing" (John 15:5). Or, as Paul puts it in 1 Corinthians 3:7, "only God ... makes things grow." Indeed, that is perhaps the best summary of the work of the Spirit in lives today. He makes the church grow, adding to it those who are being saved. He makes the Christian grow, checking our sin, strengthening our wills to obey God's Word, producing his fruit of godly character, ministering to and through the body of Christ by his gifts. The amazing reality is that God plants a seed of spiritual life in our lives and it begins to grow. Looked at another way, that seed is his life within us, in the person of the Holy Spirit, who penetrates, develops and multiplies his dynamic in every area that is open to his ministry.

What we need to remember is that sowing and growing take time. There is no overnight harvest. Similarly, there is no single experience of the Holy Spirit by which we can attain instant spiritual maturity. You don't put a baby to bed in his cot one night and expect him to be six feet tall next morning! There's a lot of growing that he has to do, and it takes time. On the other hand, a child who is not growing at all is a child who is sick and who may even be dying. Just as in the process of physical maturing there may be all sorts of ups and downs, growth spurts and more static periods, possible infections or harmful accidents, so spiritually the normal Christian life will be a similar mixture. A young child might even need surgery in order to remove a blockage which was preventing it from being nourished by a proper assimilation of food. It would be a traumatic and harrowing experience, but even when it was complete, the feeding and growing could only be gradual. We are too prone to focus on God's sometimes dramatic and emotional removal of the barriers we erect against the free flow of his Spirit in our lives, as the real work he is doing in us. But it is the regular feeding and growing that are the real work. The upheavals and special crises are simply the prelude to further growth, frequently made necessary by our own stubborn resistance.

There is no instant spiritual maturity and yet what a dynamic the life of the Spirit within us really is! It is vital, therefore, that in realising our dependence upon him, we also recognise that there is no way we can ever take over from him, or do without him, however long we may have been on the Christian pathway. God does not surrender his divine sovereignty to his creatures – even redeemed ones! Many of us have a sub-Christian experience of what we should be "in Christ", because we have left the Spirit so little room in which to operate in our lives. We have taken the controls back into our own hands and we are far too ready to tell God what he can or cannot do, in us and with us. In fact, our dependence on God has to be total. That is the only condition of spiritual health, and often he disciplines us, through testing and difficult circumstances, to bring us back to this realisation, and to regain our spiritual sense about things. We all like the easy options; it must be part of our fallen human nature. But there is no magic to lift us out of our humanity on to a spiritual "cloud nine", where we become super-spiritual. How insufferable we would be if there were! And how sad it is when Christians are desperately trying to live like that, constantly looking for a more ultimate experience than the last.

We are human; we are sinners. We always shall be this side of heaven. But our humanity is indwelt by God the Holy Spirit. Can you imagine anything more wonderful than that? There is so much more of him that we can know and experience, so much more victory over sin and the down-drag of our fallen nature, so much more holiness to be developed in our characters and behaviour. Only, let us be spiritual realists; neither idle romantics nor sceptical rationalists. That will mean allowing the Spirit to teach and guide us, as we learn to trust his promises and obey his commands.

2.

EXPERIENCING THE SPIRIT'S STRENGTH

Ezekiel 37:1-14

The hand of the LORD was upon me, and he brought me out by the Spirit of the LORD and set me in the middle of a valley; it was full of bones. He led me to and fro among them, and I saw a great many bones on the floor of the valley, bones that were very dry. He asked me, "Son of man, can these bones live?" I said, "O Sovereign LORD, you alone know." Then he said to me, "Prophesy to these bones and say to them, 'Dry bones, hear the word of the LORD! This is what the Sovereign LORD says to these bones. I will make breath enter you, and you will come to life. I will attach tendons to you and make flesh come upon you and cover you with skin; I will put breath in you, and you will come to life. Then you will know that I am the LORD.'" So I prophesied as I was commanded. And as I was prophesying, there was a noise, a rattling sound, and the bones came together, bone to bone. I looked, and tendons and flesh appeared on them and skin covered them, but there was no breath in them. Then he said to me, "Prophesy to the breath; prophesy, son of man, and say to it, 'This is what the Sovereign LORD says: Come from the four winds, O breath, and breathe into these slain, that they may live.'" So I prophesied as he commanded me, and breath entered them; they came to life and stood up on their feet – a vast army. Then he said to me: "Son of man, these bones are the whole house of Israel. They say, 'Our bones are dried up and our hope is gone; we are cut off.' Therefore prophesy and say to them: 'This is what the Sovereign LORD says: O my people, I am going to open your graves and bring you up from them; I will bring you back to the land of Israel. Then you, my people, will know that I am the LORD, when I open your graves and bring you up from them. I will put my Spirit in you and you will live, and I will settle you in your own land. Then you will know that I the LORD have spoken, and I have done it, declares the LORD.'" (Ezek. 37:1-14)

There are few passages in the Old Testament which take us more directly to the heart of the person and ministry of the Holy Spirit than this one. The name Ezekiel means "God strengthens" and the prophet's own ministry was certainly living proof of that fact. Ezekiel was a priest, taken captive to Babylon, along with King Jehoiachin and the nobility of Judah, in the great upheavals of the year 597 BC. In the fifth year of his exile he was called to be a prophet of the Lord, a ministry in which he continued for twenty-two years (593-571 BC). While Jeremiah was giving God's message in Jerusalem, Ezekiel was God's spokesman among the exiles. Much of his mysterious book is concerned with prophecies of the eventual destruction of Jerusalem, but he also foretells God's judgment on the Gentile nations. However, at chapter 33, Ezekiel begins to promise a divine work of restoration, which will involve new leadership and the return of the exiles to the promised land, to be followed by the re-construction of the cities of Judah, especially Jerusalem and the glory at its heart--the Lord's temple.

It is hardly surprising that such a message was met by his hearers with scepticism and sheer unbelief. As our chapter indicates, the people of God demonstrated two predominant characteristics at this time. They were spiritually despondent and this was because their hope in God was dead. So the Holy Spirit, who strengthens, allows his prophet, Ezekiel, to see things from God's viewpoint. And what he saw not only had relevance for his own generation, but was written for our learning. Here are spiritual principles for the people of God in every generation, including our own. As Paul reminded the Romans, the Old Testament Scriptures were written so that we might be strengthened to persevere and so we too might have hope in the everlasting Lord (Rom. 15:4).

The details of Scripture are always significant. Verse 1 stresses that this whole episode was something initiated by God himself. He gives to the man he has chosen a vision of what he is going to do. There is a double stress in verse 1 on both the powerful hand of the Lord and the powerful life of the Spirit bringing Ezekiel to the point where he is able to receive God's message. He is back in the valley or plain (the same word is used as in 3:22) which was the place where he had received his initial vision of the majesty of God at the start of his ministry. But now the picture is astonishingly different. The valley is full of bones, bleached white by the sun. They are very many and they are very dry (v. 2). It represents a battlefield turned graveyard, containing a decimated army; slaughtered but unburied. This represents the ultimate shame and curse of the ancient world--to have no one to care for you in death so that your skeleton is picked clean by the scavengers. The situation appears to be beyond all remedy. This is the nation of Israel (v. 11) as God sees them – dead and despondent. They have lost all hope. A literal translation would be "we are cut off to ourselves", which we might express as we have only ourselves to rely on. The attitude of the people is that Ezekiel's prophecies are just wishful thinking. Either God is no longer interested in them, or worse, he is no longer able to help them. Perhaps he really had been defeated by the gods of Babylon and such faith as they had in him had been a delusion. There seems to be no possibility of the situation changing. They were simply condemned to live out the consequences of their unfaithfulness.

But now let's turn our attention to God's representative. Ezekiel was not only a prophet who spoke for God to the people, but also a priest who spoke for the people to God. In verse 3, the Lord has a challenging question for him, "Can these bones live?" They were very dry. Every rule of common sense, logic and experience has to say, "No". But Ezekiel knew enough about the LORD to recognise that he is Sovereign over everything and that with God nothing is impossible. Bishop John Taylor comments, "He had the knowledge not to deny God's ability, but he lacked the faith to believe in it". Nevertheless, Ezekiel reveals his own spiritual maturity by referring the whole impossible situation to God's greater wisdom and power. "O Sovereign LORD, you alone know" (v. 3). Isn't that just where many of us find ourselves today? So God intervenes with two specific instructions. They are the means by which God's Spirit can restore a dead, despondent people into a living, confident, active army, filled with the Holy Spirit, the breath of God's life.

It happens in two stages. First, the prophet addresses the dry bones with the Word of the Lord – the word of promise (vv. 4-6). This has an immediate effect. Before Ezekiel's eyes the scattered bones are reformed into individual skeletons, which are then covered with skin and flesh; but, as yet, they are still lifeless. Stage two sees Ezekiel obediently prophesying to the breath, or wind, and as the wind breathes into the dead bodies, they live again and become once more a vast and powerful army (vv. 9-10).

Clearly the key to understanding this passage lies in the spiritual significance of these two instructions to Ezekiel. So let's examine them.

'PROPHESY TO THESE BONES' (V. 4)

Here is a vitally important principle of all real spiritual life and progress. The first command means that what God uses to bring about new life is always his own Word. "Hear the Word of the Lord" is the command to the dry bones. That is why the activity of the Holy Spirit in Scripture is always very closely linked with the Word of God. He is its original and controlling author. "Holy men of God wrote as they were moved along by Holy Spirit" (2 Peter 1:21) As we saw in chapter 1, the Word is the verbal expression of the mind and character of the invisible God. Just as our breath is expressive of our life, and we use it to articulate the thoughts of our minds to others, through the medium of speech, so the Spirit, or breath, of God is the manifestation of God's life and the expression of His mind and will. This Word of the Lord is therefore both living and lasting, in that it reflects the character of the God who spoke it.

This Word of God is also creative. It was so from the beginning. God spoke and it was done. "Let there be light and there was light" (Gen. 1:3) Inherent in the Word of God there is its own power of self-realisation. This means that if God promises something, then that Word is in itself the agent by which God will ensure that the promise is fulfilled. As Ezekiel addresses the dead bones, the Word of God is itself the life-giving creative power to bring them to life. Simply to declare God's truth on its own can never be enough. We are being shown that there is a limit to what the ministry of the most obedient prophet or faithful preacher can achieve, without the breath of the Holy Spirit. Not that we are artificially to separate Word and Spirit, for the Spirit inspired the Word and still uses it as his chief tool in bringing dead souls to life. Yet the story of past special manifestations of the Spirit in the great revivals surely serves to indicate how a faithful ministry can come alive in a new way and bring many people to life, when the Spirit comes in power upon the Word. So, back in Ezekiel's day, it was the promises of God (vv. 5-6) which led his people to a new recognition of the person and power of their God. The resurrection of the bare skeletons yields the profound result that God's people recognise anew that the LORD is sovereign and that it is only his breath or Spirit who can give life. This is not simply a bio-chemical miracle; it is representative of new spiritual life too. It is still by his self-revelation in Scripture that God's people come to know their Lord, and knowing God is eternal life (John 17:3). God's Word does the work, because as the Word of God, it alone has the authority and life-giving power of God to transform the situation. This then was the first factor in God's great work of radical change in his people. But even so, the effect was limited for the hearers were still dead men.

However, this pattern of the Word of God having within itself the executive authority and power to bring about God's will is seen even more clearly in the New Testament parallels, which centre on Jesus and his apostles. It is no surprise to find that in the ministry of Jesus it is his Word of power which accomplishes his works of compassion. Very often he would heal simply by speaking the Word, but this is especially so in the resurrections which he performed. Jairus' twelve year old daughter is brought to life by his gentle word, "Little girl, wake up". Lazarus, who has already been dead four days is summoned back by the powerful cry, "Lazarus, come out". As Charles Wesley expressed it so memorably, "He speaks, and listening to his voice, new life the dead receive". That is the power of God's life giving Word, and we must never forget it. It brings the dead to life.

Not surprisingly, the day of Pentecost and the beginning of the apostolic ministry replicate and underline the same divine pattern. Immediately before the Lord's ascension he gives to his gathered disciples the promise of power to enable them to fulfil his commission as verbal witnesses to his person and work (Acts 1:8). When the Spirit comes upon them, his power is evidenced precisely in the fulfilment of the promise as they speak the Word of God. "All of them were filled with the Holy Spirit and began to speak in other tongues as the Spirit enabled them (Acts 2:4). As Peter's declaration of the gospel proceeds, he identifies the gift of the Spirit as the fulfilment of Joel's prophecy that all of God's people will speak his prophetic word, with the specific end that "everyone who calls on the name of the Lord will be saved" (Acts 2:17-21). It is hardly surprising, then, that as God's word of gospel truth is preached that day in the life-giving power of the Holy Spirit three thousand were saved and "added to their number" (Acts 2:41). The pattern was established through Ezekiel and it has never been rescinded since. So, if we are to know a fresh movement of spiritual regeneration in our own context of equivalent deadness and human inability, it will happen only through a total dependence on the word of God to do the work of God, in the power of the same Spirit of God.

PROPHESY TO THE BREATH (V. 9)

We need to note that the one Hebrew word (ruach) is translated by three different English words in this passage. In verse 1 and again in verse 14 it is "Spirit"; in verses 5, 6, 8, 9, 10 "breath", and in verse 9 "wind(s)". But it is the same original word every time and it indicates the being or Spirit of God, in all His life-giving activity. The answer to the deadness Ezekiel encountered was a new experience of the life of God in the souls of men and women, and that must always be a sovereign work of the Holy Spirit. Without the Spirit of life, the army will remain as corpses, even though all their faculties may be restored. The only source of true spiritual life is the Holy Spirit. Sometimes he comes as a roaring gale; sometimes as a gentle whisper.

But, without him there can be no spiritual life or movement. So Ezekiel's second task is to invoke the life-giving spirit, in what is really an expression of believing prayer, in the name of the Lord, on the basis of the promise which God has already revealed (vv. 9-10).

Ezekiel asks the Spirit to breathe new life into the nation, just as God originally breathed into Adam the breath of life and he became a living soul. The effect is a miracle. So the Word and the Spirit are inseparable and without either there can be no renewing work or spiritual progress. The constant stress on the sovereignty of God underlines this vitally important lesson. What does Ezekiel have to do to bring about this revival? He simply obeys what God tells him, down to the last letter. It is God's initiative, God's agency, and God's dynamic. Indeed, Ezekiel only has a part in it because God chooses that things should be that way, and in the end his part is simply to do as he is told. Why does God arrange things in that way? Verses 13-14 tell us. "Then you, my people, will know that I am the LORD, when I open your graves and bring you up from them. I will put my Spirit in you and you will live, and I will settle you in your own land. Then you will know that I the LORD have spoken, and I have done it, declares the LORD". Such a method demonstrates the power and authority of the Lord, affirms that he is Lord of all and demands our total surrender and worship.

We do not have to look very far to see how relevant all this is to our contemporary situation. We need to face the realism that this stirring and challenging chapter presents to us. At present, in many parts of the Western world, which was once called Christendom, the church is not a vast army. Frequently, we have to confess that it looks more like a valley of dry bones. The tide of secularism sweeps our culture further and further away from any Christian moorings it once had, and we Christians seem comparatively powerless and ineffective to do anything. Of course, I am not wanting to underestimate, still less denigrate, the good things that are happening through the spread of the Gospel today. But in the western church, at any rate, it is still in most places "a day of small things." The Christian faith is not penetrating and transforming the secular culture in any notable ways. We are not to despise it (Zech. 4:10) but neither are we to be content with it. In one sense there is nothing more terminally complacent than a valley of bleached bones!

Can God make dry bones live? We have such a tiny understanding of his powerful resources. Our Christian lives are often so lethargic; we expect so little. We judge by what we've seen and heard, rather than by what God promises, and so we become the prisoners of our own limited experiences. We need to put ourselves into Ezekiel's shoes and try honestly to answer God's probing question. Do we believe the dry bones can live? Can we imagine a vast army of spiritually alive Christians actually penetrating our culture again, and making a difference for Christ, in our largely godless society? Perhaps our reply is honestly like Ezekiel's, "O Lord, you know". Yes, I know it's possible in theory but, no, I find it hard to imagine. So what is the way forward? Obedient proclamation and receiving of God's Word is what has always brought the dead to life. But with this there must also be a conscious and active dependence on God, the Holy Spirit, which cries out for Him to breathe on us.

In the sixth chapter of Ephesians, Paul identifies two great offensive weapons for our spiritual warfare (most of the armour is defensive). They are the sword of the Spirit which is the Word of God and the weapon of all prayer. We may preach the Word, but do we cry for the Spirit's strength and life? We must take the promises of God, in Scripture, and call on God, the giver of life, to fulfil them. Prayer is the end of self-confidence. As long as we believe that we, somehow, have some spiritual life in and of ourselves, we shall pray only perfunctorily. But when we begin to see the situation with God's eyes, we then begin to realise how much we need to cast ourselves on Him. "Then you will know that I the LORD have spoken, and I have done it, declares the LORD" (v. 14b). We worship a God who speaks and who acts, according to His own unchanging character. He is the Lord, the giver of life. Deadness and despondency are not the ultimate in his purposes for his people. They may be a necessary ingredient in His plan to bring us to our spiritual senses, but they are not the end of the road. Ezekiel's vision reminds us of the encouragement given to us by the Lord Jesus. "How much more will God give the Holy Spirit to those who ask him!" (Luke 11:13).

As we study Scripture's teaching about the ministry of the Holy Spirit, what will make a difference is not just more knowledge about the Word, or more understanding for the mind. They are essential as the foundation ingredient, for without them we cannot trust and obey the Lord. But things will start to change in our lives, our churches, our society, when what we know in theory drives us, in practice, to pray; to plead with God that He will breathe life into our dry bones and that the church of Jesus Christ will prove to be a mighty army, once again, in our generation. We need to start praying for that daily, now.

3.

KNOWING THE SPIRIT'S PRESENCE

Acts 1:1-8

"In my former book, Theophilus, I wrote about all that Jesus began to do and to teach until the day he was taken up to heaven, after giving instructions through the Holy Spirit to the apostles he had chosen. After his suffering, he showed himself to these men and gave many convincing proofs that he was alive. He appeared to them over a period of forty days and spoke about the kingdom of God. On one occasion, while he was eating with them, he gave them this command: "Do not leave Jerusalem, but wait for the gift my Father promised, which you have heard me speak about. For John baptised with water, but in a few days you will be baptised with the Holy Spirit." So when they met together, they asked him, "Lord are you at this time going to restore the kingdom to Israel?" He said to them: "It is not for you to know the times or dates the Father has set by his own authority. But you will receive power when

the Holy Spirit comes on you; and you will be my
witnesses in Jerusalem, and in all Judea and Samaria,
and to the ends of the earth." (Acts 1:1-8)

In the midst of all the current debate, and frequent confusion,
about the person and work of the Holy Spirit, much is rightly
made of the events of the Day of Pentecost recorded in Acts
chapter 2. The wind, the fire and the languages all contributed
their amazing and dramatic impact. It is hardly surprising that
contemporary Christians are often caught gazing wistfully
over their shoulders to that historic occasion and wishing
for "another Pentecost". Was it a once-for-all event, or is it
repeatable today? Should every Christian have a similarly
unforgettable experience? Whole theologies have been built on
Acts 2 and subsequent passages to answer these questions. But
we often seem to forget that the book begins with chapter 1
and it is only logical to remember that if we don't read and
understand the first chapter clearly, we shall be much less likely
to make consistent Biblical sense of the second chapter. Chapter
1 is also unique in that it contains words of our Lord Jesus
Christ, not recorded in any of the four gospels, but vital to our
understanding of the ministry of the Holy Spirit in our lives
today. So let's see what we need to learn from the comments Dr
Luke makes in introducing his record of the life and expansion
of the early church.

A Principle To Grasp (vv. 1-2)

Luke tells us that he is beginning the second volume of a single
work. He dedicates it to Theophilus (a man dear to God) as he
does his gospel, in order to ensure that he (and others) will have
a reliable account of the historical foundations of Christian
faith. The Acts of the Apostles starts by stating an underlying
principle, by which all that follows must be interpreted. It is
contained in the words "began" (v. 1) and "through the Holy
Spirit" (v. 2). The earthly ministry of Jesus, including the cross

and the resurrection, recorded in the gospels, was only the beginning. In every generation, Christ's work in the world has continued through the church, which is his body, animated by his risen life. And in that continuing mission every Christian has a part to play.

But Luke then immediately points out that Jesus' earthly ministry was carried out through the Holy Spirit. The Lord Jesus was making this same point himself when he told his critics, "I drive out demons by the Spirit of God" (Matt 12:28), or when he announced to the synagogue congregation in Nazareth "The Spirit of the Lord is upon me, because he has anointed me to preach good news to the poor" (Luke 4:18). Both his wonderful words and his mighty deeds were made effective through the power of the Holy Spirit. Indeed, even his redemptive work was dependent on the same enabling. "The blood of Christ, who through the eternal Spirit offered himself unblemished to God will cleanse our consciences from acts that lead to death, so that we may serve the living God" (Heb 9:14). Jesus Christ, as man, found it necessary to depend upon the Holy Spirit in and for every aspect of his ministry. How much more then does his body on earth need the anointing and enabling of the same "Paraclete", the one who is "called alongside to help"? Right at the outset of volume two, Luke inseparably links the work of Jesus with the work of the Holy Spirit.

The Holy Spirit is Jesus at work in the continuation of his ministry. "Another Comforter" (John 14:16) means another of the same sort, of the same nature, – another Jesus, we might say. The deity of the Holy Spirit is thus firmly established. And we are to understand that the Acts of the Apostles might perhaps be better entitled "The acts of the Holy Spirit through the apostles" since the extension of the ministry begun by the Lord Jesus is now continued through them by his Spirit. There is therefore no doctrine of a work of the Holy Spirit separated from the work of Jesus anywhere in the New Testament. The Spirit takes the things of Christ and makes them real and living

– he applies Christ's work to the individual. It is he who indwells Christian people to make us more like Jesus, but always on the grounds of what Christ accomplished at Calvary, and always with the purpose of exalting the Lord Jesus (John 15:26).

A PROMISE TO BELIEVE (vv. 4-5)

"You will be baptised with the Holy Spirit." What did Jesus mean by that? First, we should note that this baptism is promised in each of the four gospels (Matt. 3:11, Mark 1:7-8, Luke 3:16, John 1:33). On each occasion, John the Baptist is recorded as pointing to Jesus as the one who will baptise, not with water, but with the Holy Spirit. John claims that this was revealed to him by God, when he saw the Holy Spirit come down in the form of a dove and remain on Jesus, at his water baptism. So it's very important. Actually, the promise here in verse 5 is passive. It is something that will happen to his hearers, not because they make it happen by their effort, but because Christ promises it as a gracious gift, by his Sovereign will. "I am going to send you what my Father has promised, but stay in the city until you have been clothed with power from on high" (Luke 24:49). The emphasis is not on human achievement, but on the divine gift, coming down from God, which brings us what would otherwise be entirely beyond our reach.

Is there nothing, then, that the disciples have to do? Jesus is crystal clear in his instructions in verse 4 – "Do not leave, but wait". The only condition of the baptism is geographical. The emphasis is on Jerusalem, in the original text, but not on the waiting. We are to understand that the apostles did not secure the Holy Spirit because they waited in prayer, but because he is "the gift of my Father" (v. 4). The reception of the Holy Spirit is therefore not an opportunity, a responsibility, or even a privilege to be claimed, but the promise of a free gift of God's grace. Wherever promise is used in the New Testament, it is always contrasted with human effort. Peter makes the same point in his Pentecost address "Repent and be baptised, every one of you, in the name of Jesus Christ so that your sins may be forgiven. And you will receive the gift of the Holy Spirit. The promise is for you and your children and for all who are far off – for all whom the Lord our God will call" (Acts 2:38-39).

The baptism of the Holy Spirit then is receiving the free gift of God's grace, personally. God himself comes to take up residence in the redeemed personality of everyone who trusts in Christ as Saviour and Lord. The life of God planted in the human soul, through the person of the indwelling Spirit, is the gift of the Father made to every believer, without cost, condition or exception. As F.D. Bruner pointed out in his *Theology of the Holy Spirit*, in every passage in Acts where people become Christians they are described as receiving the Holy Spirit (the two are synonymous), and the Holy Spirit is always referred to as either the "promise" or the "gift". That is why in verse 5 there is no "may be". Jesus does not tell his disciples that if they have emptied themselves enough of their sin or self-centredness, or if they are holy enough, or if they have waited long enough, then they will receive the Spirit. His promise is uncompromising and unconditional – "you will". On the day of Pentecost, the Spirit was given, not to a few disciples who had fulfilled certain conditions, but to all (Acts 2:1-4).

We do not have to empty ourselves in order to be filled. The Father's love gift overflows to all his children. There is no record in Acts of any Christian believer either alone, or in a group or church, failing to receive the Holy Spirit, or only partly receiving. In fact, because the Holy Spirit is a person, it is impossible to receive him in bits, or by instalments! Undivided, he comes to every believer as God's free gift of grace. Neither is there any reference in Acts to the amount of faith, or even the depth of obedience, of the individual who receives the Spirit. The Spirit's work is the work of Jesus; the Spirit's title is "the Father's Promise".

To 'baptise' means literally to immerse, usually in water. It was often used to mean to cleanse thoroughly. Here the idea is the pouring out of the Holy Spirit from on high, by God, and in Acts 2:38 this is especially associated with the forgiveness of sins. So every Christian finds that this promise is still fulfilled when he or she turns to the Lord. That is what becoming a Christian, or experiencing the new birth, is all about. Deeply cleansed by the blood of Jesus, we are immersed in the life of the Holy Spirit. He becomes the new environment in which we live and move as Christians. "You are controlled not by the sinful nature but by the Spirit, if the Spirit of God lives in you. And if anyone does not have the Spirit of Christ, he does not belong to Christ" (Rom. 8:9). Let us grasp Paul's logic. Do you belong to Christ? Are you a Christian? Then the Holy Spirit is within you. There is no other way in which you could be a Christian. You have been made alive spiritually, you live in his environment, you have been initiated, or baptised, into his life. So Christians do not need to pray for the Holy Spirit, but rather to believe God's promise, and live in the enjoyment of His resources.

But this strong Biblical emphasis on the baptism of the Spirit being synonymous with becoming a Christian sometimes appears to be contradicted, or at least modified, by an individual's experience. Many testify to a "second blessing" after their conversion, marked by a fuller recognition of Jesus as Lord and a more complete commitment of the whole of one's life to him. This may be accompanied with deep emotional intensity and sometimes with physical manifestations of particular gifts. How does a Biblical understanding relate to such claims?

It will always be true that a person with an experience is never at the mercy of one with an argument and that there is no point in attempting to deny what have been real events in someone else's life. The mistake, however, is to use the experience as the foundation of theology, rather than the revelation of Scripture. Anyone's understanding of any such experience, whether one's own or someone else's, is bound to be limited, partial and finite, because we are all imperfect human beings with inadequate and distorted perceptions, who are far more culturally-conditioned than we are usually prepared to admit. It is not the factuality of the experience, but the inferences which are drawn from it which can be so misleading. As soon as my experience becomes the norm and I teach that you must have the same experience, perhaps in exactly the same way, ultimate authority has shifted from God's revealed will in Scripture, to me; from the divine to the merely human. Even though I may seek to authenticate the validity of that experience by attaching a Biblical label to it (such as "baptism in the Spirit"), necessarily that does not mean that I have understood the Biblical concept properly and it certainly cannot give me any authority to over-ride the clear teaching of Scripture, such as we have been examining, without moving the pole of authority for the whole of my Christian life away from the Bible to me and my experience.

Of course there are experiences which every Christian must have. "You must be born again" (John 3:7) is the first. "Be filled with the Spirit" (Eph. 5:18) is another, which we shall explore in detail in a later chapter. But unless that experience is commanded in Scripture, I have absolutely no right to impose what I have experienced on you, or extra-Biblical "teaching" from a particular church or sub-group on the whole body of Christ. That is just spiritual imperialism and can provide no sure ground for the theology of practical Christian living, which we all need to know and which is actually the substance of so many of the New Testament letters.

Christians all need to experience, and long for, more and more of the blessings of God, which are ours through faith in Jesus. We should be all in favour not just of a second blessing, but a third, a fourth, a fifth – an infinity of blessings stretching on into eternity. And this is often what God is doing through the unusual experiences and awarenesses of his love and grace, which all believers know from time to time. Sometimes, their emotional intensity is associated with a fresh repentance, in an area of life where we have been resistant and rebellious. Often they draw from us a deeper consecration and a renewed obedience. God deals with each of his children sovereignly, according to his will and our needs. What we must not do is go beyond what is written and seek to impose what is an individual and personal experience as the norm for our fellow Christians.

A POWER TO APPROPRIATE (VV. 6-8)

Like the disciples, we too can so easily become preoccupied with the wrong priorities in our Christian lives. They were still obsessed about an earthly kingdom with all its trappings of human power and influence. In the Gospels we find them so often turning aside from the main issues of Jesus' teaching to some tangent of their personal speculation. But aren't we just like them? We too become more interested in the gifts than the giver, or in our power rather than in his purposes. Gently, but firmly, Jesus re-directs them (v. 7). Times or dates are God's preserve, not ours, and we are not to waste our energies on idle speculation. Jesus promises that they will receive power, but it will be neither political nor temporal. There is something very different at the heart of God's purposes for His people.

Jesus diverts their attention to his plan for world-wide mission, which is the means by which the kingdom will spread and which becomes the major theme of Luke's book. It has been rightly said that verse 8 is really the contents page of the book of Acts. It sets out the agenda for all that is to follow. Once again, Jesus gives them a clear straightforward promise. "You will receive power... you will be my witnesses". The power is the Holy Spirit in person; not an influence, but God himself. The word translated "power" (dunamis) means the ability to get a job done. In this case, the job is the world-wide spread of Christ's kingdom. That is the Spirit's primary work in the world.

Once again, Jesus stresses that the Spirit will come upon them, the symbolism teaching that the Spirit is the gift of the heavenly Father, sent from above. He is not dependent on our inner state. We do not deserve him, or generate his presence in our lives. Rather, he comes upon us from above, just because he is God, and in our relationship with him lies our experience of his divine power. It is not power for its own sake, or even for ours. The power is for the accomplishment of God's purposes in other people's lives. That is what lies behind the commission to be "my witnesses". In the original my is emphatic, and that is significant. As with the apostles, so the purpose of the Holy Spirit's presence in any believer's life is not to witness to that individual's gifts, or power, or experiences, but to witness through that Christian, to the world, about Jesus. That was the original call of Christ and it is still a touchstone by which to measure whether any experience is genuinely of the Holy Spirit.

We are being taught here that the power inherent in the baptism of the Holy Spirit is primarily a power which unites us to Christ. "You will receive... and you will be". The power is seen most clearly not in what we do, but in what we are. There is a sense in which this promise was unique to the apostles. What gave them their unrepeatable authority was that they were personal eye-witnesses of the resurrected Christ, who personally commissioned them to go and tell. We have become believers on the basis of their testimony. But there is a secondary sense in which all true believers, in every generation, have been called to follow in their footsteps. At the heart of our Christian faith is the testimony of our experience of the risen Lord also, although our eyes have not literally seen him nor have our ears heard his voice. Nevertheless we too are called to be his witnesses, in our own limited way. To quote F.D. Bruner again, "The power of the Holy Spirit is his ability to join men and women to the risen Christ so that they are able to represent Him. There is no higher blessing". There could be no greater privilege.

The apostles, then, were eye-witnesses of Christ's ministry, death and resurrection, in a unique sense. Almost all the other references to "witness" in Acts are linked to the resurrection. But even for them, it was only when the Spirit had come that they "went everywhere, preaching Jesus." The important point to note is that Christ was central to all they did. Whenever the Holy Spirit baptises a new believer into the body of Christ, the Lord Jesus becomes the central ingredient of his or her testimony. The emphasis will not then be on pushing others through the hoops of my personal experience, but on introducing others to my Saviour. He deals with each of us individually. And as the book of Acts unfolds, it becomes increasingly clear that this is how the gospel spreads. What begins with Jews in Jerusalem spreads to Judea and Samaria (Acts 8:1), God confirming his work with special and exceptional signs. By chapter 10 Peter is sent to the Gentile centurion, Cornelius, and the Holy Spirit falls on all who hear his message (Acts 10:44). In chapter 13, Paul and Barnabas are sent out from the church at Antioch and the Gentile mission has begun. As Paul later explained, in Galatians 3:14, "Christ redeemed us in order that the blessing given to Abraham might come to the Gentiles through Christ Jesus, so that by faith we might receive the promise of the Spirit." This is the same Spirit who today lives within us, through faith in Christ as our Saviour, and whose power is still to be appropriated by the same trust and obedience.

If we can grasp this reality it will save us from making the mistake of endlessly seeking for "more power", as though this was somehow a distinct and separate reality from the indwelling Spirit. Powerful Christians are not those who are plugged in to a secret energy-supply, which they have somehow persuaded God to grant them as a sort of spiritual elite. This is to go back to the fallacy that we could have more of the Spirit than the Spirit we already have.

When we see other believers who seem to be more full of power than we think we are, because they appear to be better witnesses, or to live more godly lives, or to have a more acute awareness of the presence of God, it is very tempting to go looking for what they have got, which we "ordinary" Christians don't seem to have. There are conferences, books, videos, whole ministries dedicated to providing the "answer". But Scripture teaches us that every Christian, indwelt by God's Spirit, is already in possession of the greatest spiritual dynamic possible – the Lord himself. There is no extra superior resource available or needed. The normal Christian life is constantly to be "strengthened with all power according to his glorious might" (Col. 1:11). The supply is surely available; but it is faith which plugs us in, and that is where the real challenge lies. There is no lack in God's power; the problem is that we fail to trust and obey, to believe his promises and so to be empowered to fulfil his command.

Are you a Christian? Then the Holy Spirit is within you. But why has he been given? Acts tells us that he is our ability to become like the Lord Jesus, as he brings all the resources of Christ's risen life into our experience. He wants to use our lives, in our generation, as witnesses to the reality of the gospel, which we have believed because of the apostolic testimony. Many of us know we lack power, but it is not because of any shortage in God's supply. Rather, it is because we quench, or grieve, the Holy Spirit. We refuse to allow him to control certain areas of our lives. If we have no heart for mission, it must be because we are not appropriating the gracious gift of the Holy Spirit. We need to be honest about our own spirituality, before God. Is there developing in us a conspicuous and recognisable likeness to Jesus? That is the true mark of the Spirit's work. God is not interested in providing us with a fragrant bubble-bath of spiritual ecstasy, but in our daily growing in grace, our daily concern for lost people and our daily readiness and availability to be a witness for Christ.

What a daunting, impossible task it must have seemed for this little group of despised men, to be claiming the whole world for Christ! But they went out and did it. Why? Surely it was because they believed the promise, and so they appropriated the power of the Holy Spirit, as their ability to get the job done. Today, the living church of Christ in our land numbers many hundreds of thousands and all around the world its numbers are growing. Our message is the same; our resources are undiminished. Is our faith not equal to theirs?

4.

RECOGNISING THE SPIRIT'S WORK

JOHN 16:5-16

"Now I am going to him who sent me, yet none of you asks me, 'Where are you going?'" Because I have said these things, you are filled with grief. But I tell you the truth: It is for your good that I am going away. Unless I go away, the Counsellor will not come to you; but if I go, I will send him to you. When he comes, he will convict the world of guilt in regard to sin and righteousness and judgment: in regard to sin, because men do not believe in me; in regard to righteousness, because I am going to the Father, where you can see me no longer; and in regard to judgment, because the prince of this world now stands condemned. I have much more to say to you, more than you can now bear. But when he, the Spirit of truth, comes, he will guide you into all truth. He will not speak on his own; he will speak only what he hears, and he will tell you what is yet to come. He will bring glory to me by taking from what is mine

and making it known to you. All that belongs to the
Father is mine. That is why I said the Spirit will take
from what is mine and make it known to you. "In a
little while you will see me no more, and then after a
little while you will see me." (John 16:5-16)

The teaching of our Lord Jesus Christ in the Gospels should
always command our most serious attention, and nowhere is
that more so than when he is instructing his disciples about the
ministry of the Holy Spirit and his future plans for their lives
and witness. So, we need to keep before us the setting of this
very important passage in order to understand its full impact.

From chapter 13 of John's Gospel onwards, the Lord Jesus
has been preparing his disciples for his imminent departure.
He has predicted his betrayal; but then he has counter-balanced
that by giving them the promise that another "Comforter" will
be sent to strengthen them. He has taught them that although
the time will come when they will not see him any more, in his
earthly body, yet their relationship to him will be as real and as
fruitful as that of vine branches which are vitally connected to
a central vine stem. All the branches have to do to be fruitful is
to keep remaining in the vine, and the disciples must similarly
abide in Christ, maintaining their vital connection with him, by
faith. Then they will be able to continue asking him for all they
need and loving one another fervently. This teaching takes on
a special importance and urgency because the world is going to
hate them just as it hates their master. Persecution will come;
of that they can be sure. But they must not give up. Rather, they
must continue to testify, which is one of the main reasons why
the Holy Spirit will be given to them.

How did the disciples react to all this? Verses 5 and 6, at the
start of our passage, give us a hint. They were numbed by the
news. Their questions seem to have dried up. This avalanche
of information was beginning to have an effect on them as
they considered its implications. They were overwhelmed with
grief and sorrow. Jesus realised that they could not cope with

any more at that stage (v. 12). What he had told them was like a heavy load that bowed their backs, or like black storm clouds that filled their horizons. The positives he had taught them about the coming of the Holy Spirit and the joy of abiding in Christ faded. They could only see the despair involved in being bereft of Christ's presence (v. 6).

It is a great encouragement in these circumstances to see the sensitive reaction of the Lord Jesus to their changing mood and need. He knows all about our own reactions too and he never allows us to be overloaded. I sometimes think that Christ-likeness, which is another way of describing the fruit of the Spirit, is most clearly seen in Christians today through our sensitivity to one another, in our realising the effects which our words or actions have on one another. The hasty, thoughtless word, the unkind jibe, the hostile reaction or the cold snub are so unlike the Lord Jesus Christ. And yet how often they characterise Christian relationships and reactions. We hurt one another so much by the way we speak, or by the letters we write because we are still so self-centred. Every time our inner motivation is a personal reaction "I'll show him", or "I'll give him a piece of my mind", we need to " watch out!" Such thinking is not the mind of Christ!

Do you remember how Isaiah describes the Spirit-filled servant of the Lord (Is. 42:2)? "He will not shout or cry out, or raise his voice in the streets. A bruised reed he will not break and a smouldering wick he will not snuff out." That is the character of our Saviour. Are we anything like him? Of course we rejoice that we can be ourselves before him and that we do not have to pretend to be better than we are. There is nothing, anyway, that we can hide from his perfect knowledge. Sadly, our reactions are all too often self-centred or self-pitying, but he knows, understands and is willing to forgive. What we have to realise, however, is that he does not condone them. Instead, he begins to instruct us as to why things are as they are, and then show us God's path through our wrong reactions to a better way.

One of the saddest experiences is to meet Christians who have become stuck in the concrete of their own self-preoccupation, becoming more and more critical of others, because they will not let the Lord teach them, at a deep, life-changing level. They resist the Spirit's correction and condemn themselves to a moribund spiritual existence.

So, Jesus makes an astonishing, but categorical, statement in verse 7. Far from conspiring with their self-pity, although he fully understands their reaction, in fact he explodes it with a stunning truth, which will totally change their perspective. It is actually better for him to go, because the blessings that the counsellor will bring to his disciples will far outweigh the physical presence of Jesus, in his human body. After all, he was limited to one geographical location, and to one point of time in history. The disciples might not like what he is telling them, but his Word is truth, which they and we need to believe. If he says it is best for him to go, it is.

For ourselves, this means that we do not need to look back wistfully to first century Israel and wish that we could have seen him then, or heard his voice, as though somehow that would make us stronger Christians. The truth which explodes such nostalgic sentimentalism is that by his Spirit living within us, Jesus is with us everywhere, every day. This explains why some Christians (though not all!) find a visit to the land of Israel an anti-climax. It is a privilege and pleasure to visit the land of the book, but it can only help us to understand and know the Bible better, not to get nearer to Jesus. We could not be nearer than we are, because his Spirit is within us.

Whatever Jesus plans for his followers they can be sure that "it is for your good" (v. 7). That was a great challenge to the disciples' faith, as it is to ours when we are similarly in the dark. "Is what is happening really for my good, Lord?" "Yes, that is why I permit it". Was it not for our good that in his death on the cross, his exodus from the world, the Lord Jesus opened the door into heaven for all who trust Him? Is it not for our good that the ascended King, like a conquering general, pours out his good gifts on his people (Eph. 4:8-11). We share in the spoils of his triumphs. His greatest gift is the "counsellor" (Paraclete) whom he sends into the life of every Christian, to bring all the benefits of his divine person into every situation of our lives. Could anything be more for our good than that? The rest of this passage teaches us how that "goodness" will work out in the ministry of the Holy Spirit both in the world (vv. 8-11), and in the church (vv. 13-16).

THE HOLY SPIRIT AT WORK IN THE WORLD (VV. 8-11)

The first ingredient of the Spirit's ministry is that he will "convict" (v. 8). The word means to bring something to the light, to show it up for what it is, in its true colours. Only God, the Holy Spirit can do that because only he is perfect truth. So what does God reveal to the world? He persuades men and women of the truth about sin (v. 9). Though the details may vary, the same essential story is present in every individual's experience of conversion. The Holy Spirit works through the conscience, which is God's bridgehead into all our lives. He exposes the sinfulness of the human heart in terms of our rebellion against God. We refuse to give him the rightful place in our lives, to let God be God in the practical affairs of our daily experience, and the evidence of that is seen in the world's refusal to believe in Christ. The foundational sin of humanity is our rejection of Christ as God and therefore as the Lord of our lives. The essence of our human sinfulness is a unilateral declaration of independence from God. All the sins which we tend to classify and evaluate as being worse or less serious than others actually stem from our fundamentally wrong relationship to God, fractured by our rebellion.

The first great work of the Spirit, when he starts to deal with us, is to awaken a personal awareness of sin and guilt. We are not talking about guilt feelings, but the deep conviction that I am a rebel before God. It is one thing to admit that we are all morally flawed, after all nobody is perfect. There are plenty of people who are willing to admit that we are all made in the same mould; it's just that some are mouldier than others! But it is quite another to recognise myself as a guilty sinner, in God's eyes, who deserves nothing but his wrath and condemnation. When the Holy Spirit comes, he begins to work by bringing me to an end of my self-confidence and showing me my life as God sees it in the light of his law, which is the expression of his holy character. Only then can I recognise how much I need his power to change me.

Nor is this experience simply confined to the beginning of his work. It is always characteristic of the Spirit's continuing work in a Christian's life too. He goes on showing us layers of sin, hidden deep in our consciences, ingrained attitudes and habitual reactions which spoil and mar God's work in us and through us. It's rather like clearing out a cellar where years of junk have accumulated and begun to moulder. This explains why so many new Christians feel within a few months of their conversion that they are worse than they were before they turned to Christ, and begin to wonder whatever has gone wrong. Actually, it is a sign that everything is going right! The Holy Spirit is continuing his work of conviction, bringing sin to light, so that it can be recognised for what it is, confessed and then abandoned. The work of sanctification, making the Christian like Jesus, is well underway!

Secondly, the Spirit convicts about "righteousness" (v. 10). When I begin to recognise my own sin, the Holy Spirit then shows me, by way of total contrast, the righteousness of Christ. When he spoke these words, the Lord Jesus was about to die a criminal's death on the cross. That was how this world saw and evaluated what happened to him. But far more was entailed in the cross than that. The morally perfect life of flawless righteousness which Jesus lived in the world meant that he was able to offer his obedient will and his sinless life as an atoning sacrifice to his Father in heaven, for the sins of the whole world. He accepted all our sin and guilt, meeting the just sentence of death on our behalf, so that we might know that his perfect righteousness has been put to our account, to cover all our iniquity. Having lived the perfect life, which we have all failed to live, he died the atoning death, which we deserve to die. As Paul explains in 2 Corinthians 5:21, "God made him who had no sin to be sin for us, so that in him we might become the righteousness of God." But once that death had been accomplished, the guarantee that his atoning sacrifice was indeed accepted by the Father was seen in the glorious resurrection of his beloved Son, on the third day. Having been raised, the victorious Lord ascended to heaven, as supreme conqueror, to whom the highest place belongs by sovereign right. Only those who are righteous can appear before God in heaven, but that is where Jesus is. So the Holy Spirit's work in the world is to reveal who Christ is in his perfect righteousness, as the only one who can deal with the problem of human sin and rebellion. Then he implants the conviction that the death of this Lord Jesus is the only way by which a sinner can ever be made right before a holy God.

Thirdly, the convicting work of the Spirit is about "judgment" (v. 11). The cross spells the judgment and defeat of the devil and of all the forces of evil that are ranged against God and his human creation. Satan is called the "prince of this world", because the world largely follows his delusions, rejecting God's salvation in Christ. That is why the world is condemned, and comes under God's judgment, which must issue in the eternal separation of those who have refused him from the God of grace. Hell is a dreadful and eternal reality.

How are people in our century ever to believe such things? Not by human cleverness, or persuasion. When the Spirit comes, his work is to convict and convince – and yet the human heart so readily quenches, grieves and resists him. But let's think of the application personally. Take time to remember what God has done by his Spirit already, and continues to do, in your life and mine. The work of the Holy Spirit is to bring me to an end of myself and my imagined self-sufficiency, living for number one. He reveals to me my sin, Christ's righteousness and God's judgment and brings me to realise that only in Christ can forgiveness, release and freedom be found. When the Spirit comes, he moves me to turn to Christ in faith to experience salvation and forgiveness, so that His righteousness may be put to my account and I may be justified before God. He reveals my spiritual bankruptcy, so that I begin to see the desperate need I have for the riches of his righteousness which can only be appropriated by faith. This is the great work of the Holy Spirit in the world. He exalts Christ and convicts the sinner. He moves us to repent of our sin and turn to the Saviour.

As we reflect on these miracles, which have happened already in the life of every Christian, we are greatly encouraged and re-invigorated for the ongoing work of evangelism. It is so strengthening to know that as we take the gospel out into the world, the sovereign Spirit of God is at work in all sorts of hidden ways, quite unknown to us, in the lives of those with whom we come into contact. The sovereignty of God in evangelism is the greatest possible stimulus to the church's witness to Christ, both in words and actions. If we were to think for one moment that the conversion of anyone depended on us, on our ability, or even our faithfulness, which of us would not soon be sunk in despair? But thank God it does not! It is all the work of his gracious Spirit, the wind that "blows wherever it pleases" (John 3:8), so that we can never predict when, or where, or how he will choose to begin his work of conviction leading to repentance and faith.

Not only does that make evangelism exciting, but it also lifts the burden of expectation from us to God and it reminds us that one of the ongoing ministries of the Spirit is to bring us to the end of all our confidence in the flesh, especially in our service for Christ and our testimony to the gospel. For "no-one can say, 'Jesus is Lord', except by the Holy Spirit" (1 Cor. 12:3).

It means that we can never possibly predict who will be most likely to turn, for we can only look on the outward appearance and we do not know the heart. So it means that we never give up praying, never give up loving and never give up expecting God to do this miracle of his converting grace in the lives of many more people. But what is his work in those who do turn?

THE HOLY SPIRIT AT WORK IN THE CHURCH (vv. 13-16)

These verses contain some amazing and wonderful promises which explain what the gift of the Holy Spirit means to Christian believers. In verse 13, Jesus promises that he will guide his disciples into all truth, including what is yet to come, while in the next verse we are told that he will bring glory to the Lord Jesus, by making what is his, known to followers (v. 14). These two promises are so clearly inter-connected that they really become one. For the disciples, at this stage in their development, they could only see the truth dimly, but when the Spirit came, at Pentecost and afterwards, he illuminated their minds to understand it fully. The word 'guide' is used in the Greek translation of the Old Testament to describe God leading Israel, through the desert to the promised land. It speaks of the gradual forward movement that is characteristic of pilgrimage. A major ingredient of church history is God guiding his people more fully into his truth, so that today we have the privilege of being able to understand its meaning and see its outworking more fully than the apostles could at that point in time.

The major part of the fulfilment of this promise lay in the Spirit's inspiration of the apostles as they wrote the New Testament Scriptures. But it also has a continuing, subsidiary fulfilment in the work of the Spirit teaching every generation of believers the truth; always more deeply and fully as we respond in faith and obedience. He does not reveal new truth, but leads us into the whole truth which is already set forth in Jesus. After all, there could be no fuller revelation of God's truth than in the Lord Jesus Christ. He is God's final word to mankind, "full of grace and truth". There is no clearer expression of God and nothing more to be added to it. "In Christ are hidden all the treasures of wisdom and knowledge ... in Christ all the fulness of the Deity lives in bodily form, and you have been given fulness in Christ, who is the Head over every power and authority." (Col. 2:3, 9-10). If Jesus is the Truth, obviously there can be no further truth beyond him. Just as he is the way into which the disciples must be led by the Holy Spirit, so he is the truth by which we must be guided (see John 14:6)

We need to be clear and sure about this sufficiency of divine truth in the Biblical revelation because there is so much confusion around in the contemporary church. Peter makes the point crystal clear in 2 Peter 1:3-4. "God's divine power has given us everything we need for life and godliness through our knowledge of him who called us by his own glory and goodness. Through these he has given us his very great and precious promises, so that through them you may participate in the divine nature and escape the corruption in the world caused by evil desires". The power of the Spirit is mediated through the promises of the Scripture and together they constitute all we need. They are totally sufficient. Biblical Christians are not expecting fresh revelations! They recognise that in our individual experience God has yet more light to break forth from his holy Word, as the Pilgrim Fathers expressed it. But it is from the Word already given that the light shines (2 Peter 1:19) not from an inner illumination, or some fresh "revelation". The only eternal truth that exists is the truth as it is in Jesus. The Holy Spirit does not set us free to wander into new realms of "revelation", secretly given or privately received. For the power of the Spirit is not revealed in secret, mystical messages given to a few super-spiritual people. His power is seen in the proclamation of Jesus Christ as the way, the truth and the life, through the objective realities of the Gospel, which move men and women to leave the world's side and cleave to Christ (John 14:6). The "things to come" to which Jesus is referring here (v. 13) and which he has now shown are all written in Scripture. They include the cross, the resurrection, the gift of Holy Spirit, the formation and spread of the church, the end of the age and the eternal kingdom.

To some Christians an emphasis like this tends to sound a bit abstract and detached, academic even. Surely the Spirit's work is not simply to inform us about doctrinal truth in the form of propositional revelation, is it? Doesn't he come to pour the love of God into our lives, to give us the deep assurance of unconditional acceptance in Jesus and to apply emotional balm to our wounded spirits with his peace? These are certainly valid and important questions and I would want to respond to both aspects equally positively, just as Scripture does.

One of the greatest tragedies of the past thirty years or so among evangelical Christians has been the pursuit and development of an un-Biblical dichotomy between facts and feelings, and so between the Word and the Spirit. The mistake is to emphasise one at the expense of the other, even to the extreme of virtually ignoring the other altogether. To imagine that the Word of God, doctrine, truth and the illumination of the mind are somehow antithetical to the Spirit, experience, love and the softening of the heart is a profound error. Yet it seems to have spread everywhere, when just a moment's thought about our make-up as human beings would be enough to show us that it cannot possibly be right.

We are not "just minds" or "just hearts". We are whole persons, made in the image of the God who thinks and speaks, who loves and acts, and who has made us with minds to understand his self-revelation in the words of Scripture, hearts to accept his truth and enthrone the Lord Jesus at the control-centre of the personality, and wills to put into action what we have come to understand and embrace in the gospel. Any theology of the Christian life which does not include all these elements, in their proper relationships to each other, is bound to prove seriously deficient, if not positively misleading. It was

Dr Martyn Lloyd-Jones who used to describe the preaching of the Bible as the process by which the Word of God, in the power of the Holy Spirit, first captured the mind, in order to warm the heart and then to activate the will. Unless all three are interactively involved, we cannot begin to grow to maturity in Christ.

No-one is at liberty to choose to be a "love Christian" rather than a "truth Christian", or to major on the Word without the Spirit. A merely cerebral Christianity which retreats into a spiritual ghetto of precise doctrinal definitions and abstract theoretical debate, repressive of the emotions and denying the rich experience of a relationship of love and trust with the Lord Jesus, is a travesty of New Testament faith and will soon dry up in sterile aridity. But equally, a Christianity which is only interested in a roller-coaster ride of emotional excitement, with a disdain for the truth of God's self-revelation in Scripture and an anti-intellectual bias, concentrating exclusively on feelings, pictures, inarticulate desires and responses will soon blow up in spiritual, mental and psychological exhaustion and may well destroy what roots of faith did exist. We need to determine that these extreme positions as their caricatures of one another will not be allowed to bring such division to another generation of genuine believers. We all need both the Spirit and the Word and both in the fullest possible measure, for nothing less will bring true glory to the Trinitarian God of love and unity, into whose image we are being re-made.

"He will bring glory to me by taking from what is mine and making it known to you" (v. 14). The great concern of the Holy Spirit, therefore, is to glorify Jesus, because his glory is the glory of the Father too (v. 15a). Just as the Son spoke the words the Father gave him, so the Holy Spirit takes the things of the Lord Jesus (his words, his character, his saving work) and reveals them ever more deeply and fully to his disciples, the living church. Those disciples, empowered by the Holy Spirit, then go back into the hostile world, which does not know God,

and otherwise would never want to know him, to testify of
Christ, and through that testimony to see the powerful Spirit
at work, convicting other rebels of sin, righteousness and
judgment. The Spirit came to guide Christ's followers into all
truth, to show them God's great eternal plans and what is yet to
be. In this way he glorifies Jesus, and the church glorifies Jesus
too. Then the Son, the Spirit and the church together glorify the
Father, before a lost and dying world. Anything that glorifies
men cannot therefore be the work of God. Anything that
brings glory to the Spirit, rather than the Son and the Father, is
not the Spirit's work. He is given to reveal Christ in all his glory
as the Truth, to exalt him and to lead us all to fall at his feet and
crown him king. That loving, joyful submission is the authentic
Biblical proof that the Holy Spirit really is at work in us.

This is underlined in the verses which immediately follow
our passage (vv. 17-24) where Jesus deals more fully with the
sorrow which had currently filled the disciples' hearts. Although
at this stage they did not really understand what Jesus meant by
the statements about his departure and his return, and perhaps
especially because they seem to have been inhibited about asking
him to explain (vv. 17-19), Jesus graciously reveals why their
sorrow will be turned to joy. Using the picture of childbirth, he
explains how anguish and pain are the precursors of great joy
because of the outcome in the gift of a new human life (v. 21).
He then applies the example... "so with you" (vv. 21-22a).
Their present grief and pain will be replaced by overwhelming
and constant joy, when the renewed presence of the Lord Jesus
in the person of the "Counsellor", the Holy Spirit, will bring
them complete understanding, open access to the Father and
the joy of all their needs being met and their prayers being
answered (vv. 23-24).

It is important to remember that the ultimate fruit of the
Spirit's work in the lives of all true believers is joy, so that this
is to be the predominant characteristic of the people of God
in this world. This is not a glib, facile happiness, because we

continue to live in a fallen world of sorrow and pain, which we all feel deeply. But Christians are not sorrowful people. We have a deep joy within us, because Christ lives in us here and now by his Spirit and because the blessings of the eternal kingdom are already beginning to be experienced, even in this world. As Isaac Watts put it, "The men of grace have found glory begun below". Not complete, or anything like it, but "begun". So joyless Christians are, at the very least, a contradiction in terms and worse, they can appear to be living contradictions of the gospel. As we shall see in the next chapter, the fruit of the Spirit is joy, which is one of the most infectious and attractive features of the gospel of Christ and which the watching world always needs to see more clearly and consistently experienced in the people of the good news.

5.

PRODUCING THE SPIRIT'S FRUIT

GALATIANS 5:13-26

You, my brothers, were called to be free. But do not use your freedom to indulge the sinful nature; rather, serve one another in love. The entire law is summed up in a single command: "Love your neighbour as yourself." If you keep on biting and devouring each other, watch out or you will be destroyed by each other. So I say, live by the Spirit, and you will not gratify the desires of the sinful nature. For the sinful nature desires what is contrary to the Spirit, and the Spirit what is contrary to the sinful nature. They are in conflict with each other, so that you do not do what you want. But if you are led by the Spirit, you are not under law. The acts of the sinful nature are obvious: sexual immorality, impurity and debauchery; idolatry and witchcraft; hatred, discord, jealousy, fits of rage, selfish ambition, dissensions, factions and envy; drunkenness, orgies, and the like. I warn you, as I did before, that those who live like this will not inherit the kingdom of God. But the fruit of the Spirit is love, joy, peace, patience, kindness, goodness, faithfulness, gentleness and self-control. Against such things there is no law. Those who belong to Christ Jesus have crucified the sinful nature with its passions and desires. Since we live by the Spirit, let us keep in step with the Spirit. Let us not become conceited, provoking and envying each other. (Gal. 5:13-26)

Let's imagine that we are at a great international airport at one of the boarding gates, watching the passengers about to travel thousands of miles. As they board the plane, you are likely to observe a variety of different attitudes among them. Some stride on full of confidence, hardly giving it a second thought. Others are nervous and diffident, wondering if the marvels of modern air travel will really work in their case. Some might be unable to walk for themselves and need to be wheeled on, in a chair, or even carried on a stretcher. What they eventually have in common is that they all commit themselves to the plane. They know that the laws of gravity make it impossible for a human being to fly, but they also know that the laws of aerodynamics are able to overcome the down-drag of gravity. Once they are in the plane, the thrust and energy of those great jet engines will carry them through the sky to their destination. Of course, if any passenger was to be able to remove himself from the environment of the plane, and decide he could fly without its assistance, the old law would immediately take over and down he would go. So what keeps them flying? Not the confidence with which some boarded the aircraft; nor the quality of their faith, anymore than the nervousness of others would prevent them taking off. Everything depends on the power of the engines – an objective reality, which generates the subjective experience. Only that external power can fly the passengers from A to B; but all the time the power is experienced, the "miracle" happens.

One of the great New Testament Greek words to describe the Holy Spirit is "dunamis". As we have seen, its basic meaning is the ability to get the job done, though it is frequently translated 'power' rather than 'ability'. We derive our English words dynamic and dynamite from this root. The function of dynamite is, after all, to get a job done! But this power is a person, as we have been learning. Going back to our illustration of the plane, we can see that only the power of the Spirit (like the principles of aeronautical engineering) can overcome the down-drag of our old sinful, human nature (like the law of gravity). Paul puts it this way in Romans 8:2, "Through Christ Jesus the law of the Spirit of life set me free from the law of sin and death."

But if the dynamic of the Spirit is the ability to accomplish a task, or complete a job, what is it that God wants to be done? It is to Galatians 5 that we turn for one of the clearest of all the New Testament answers. He wants to produce the fruit of the Spirit in our lives, as we grow in Christ-likeness. He wants to restore the image of God in us, which has been so marred and spoiled by our sin. He wants to make us holy, through his Spirit within us, and to re-fashion our rebellious lives into the pattern of his Son's obedient devotion to the Father's will. When that is happening, we know that it is the Holy Spirit who is at work within us, and that we are neither quenching, nor grieving him.

At this point, we need to remind ourselves again that the Holy Spirit is not the preserve of a few special Christians. The opening verses of Acts 2 which describe the giving of the Spirit to the church have a wonderful inclusiveness about them. The disciples were all together, all 120 of them, in one place (v. 1). The wind from heaven filled the whole house (v. 2). Tongues of fire came to rest on each of them (v. 3). All of them were filled with Holy Spirit (v. 4). From the very beginning, there was a universality about the Spirit's life, energising the whole church, to be the body of Christ on earth. What was created that day was not a human organisation, but a divine organism. As every

Christian is a member of the body, linked personally by faith to Christ the head, so Christ's life flows into each and every one of his redeemed people. We could not be Christians at all if we did not have the Holy Spirit within us. (Rom. 8:9).

It is also important to establish that the Holy Spirit is not given just for the Christian's own private and personal enjoyment. "We were all baptised by one Spirit into one body" Paul wrote in 1 Corinthians 12:13. There is a corporate dimension to all of God's redeeming work. The Holy Spirit is the author of unity, both through the truth which he teaches us, and also through the common life, by which he empowers us. Just as the individual Christian's body is a temple of the Holy Spirit, so the church corporately becomes the location on earth where God dwells among his people, by his Spirit. In the same way that there can be no personal salvation without the Spirit, so there can be no corporate fellowship, apart from His presence and power. It is not his work to produce spiritual "lone rangers". So we should be on our guard whenever any so-called gifts or manifestations of the Spirit do not have a direct ministry of building up the body. They are not spiritual playthings for individual Christians to enjoy as though these were the self-indulgent luxuries of Christian experience. That would simply reflect the world's way of looking at God's gracious gifts and be more pagan than Christian, in looking after "number one".

A third important factor to bear in mind is that the Holy Spirit is not confined to special dramatic experiences. Paul expresses this very clearly on three occasions in this passage. In verse 16, he tells us to "live by the Spirit". In verse 18, he speaks of Christians as being "led by the Spirit". In verse 25, he counsels us to "keep in step with the Spirit". Clearly each of these references speaks about an ongoing process, the continuous working out of what the Spirit is working in to our lives. There is also a stress upon the fact that all these initiatives for progress belong to him. So, in verse 16, he provides the resources; in verse 18, he sets the direction, and in verse 25 he controls the pace. This potential is already inherent in the gift of the Spirit, but it has to be appropriated and enjoyed by our practical faith and personal obedience. Notice that the verbs used all speak of progress, development and growth. Spiritual Christians are always moving forward. To opt for the status quo, whether personally or corporately, is to miss the adventure of life in the Spirit, and ultimately to vegetate, rather than bearing fruit. Static Christians invariably stagnate.

With these necessary correctives in mind, we can now turn to the positives which lie within the Lord's gracious purpose in sending the Holy Spirit to his people. He wants us to be so filled with him that we become really fruitful Christians. At one level, fruit-bearing is the most natural thing in the world. God has so structured and ordained his world that all life will bear fruit after its kind, unless it is prevented by hostile circumstances militating against it. So it is with the life of the Spirit and the fruit of the Spirit. This analogy of fruit-bearing actually teaches us a great deal about living the Christian life.

In nature, fruit-bearing is not an optional extra. It is the major purpose of the tree's life cycle. Fruit-bearing is not something external, added on from the outside; rather, it is the fundamental proof of the inner life. When we moved into our last home we were not entirely sure of the nature of the trees in the garden, until they bore their fruit. Then we knew which were apples and which were pears. We go to the shops at Christmas time to buy decorations with which to beautify our Christmas trees, but we know that they are not the tree's fruit. They have to be added on. But I have not yet been to the supermarket to buy apples in order to tie them on to the tree in the garden. The life within produces the fruit.

That also leads us to recognise that fruit-bearing does not happen suddenly. It takes time for the fruit to mature and ripen. All the time there is the quiet development, steadily progressing, as the hidden life within is gradually revealed more fully in the swelling fruit. Of course, the amount of fruit will depend on a number of inter-related factors including the health of the tree, the condition of the soil, and the vagaries of the climate. Fruit trees have to be looked after carefully, if they are to fulfil their potential in producing a maximum yield. There are all sorts of diseases that can blight them and they seem subject to innumerable pests. Again the analogy holds good, for our Christian lives are planted in a hostile environment, as verse 17 reminds us. Indeed, there is a contrary flow of life within the very core of our being ("the sinful nature") which can only be overcome by a superior power. That is why we must live by the Spirit. There is no other resource adequate to counteract the sinful propensities of our fallen humanity. It is not difficult to recognise someone who is responding to the Spirit's promptings and living by his energy. The unmistakable signs will always be their fragrance and their fruit.

What God is looking for in our lives is the fruit of his own life, his Spirit within. Verses 22-23 which describe the qualities produced by the Spirit within us are familiar to most Christians – perhaps too familiar. One way of coming freshly to these verses is to see them as a pen-picture of the Lord Jesus Christ himself. They are not just nine loosely-related virtues, but one integrated character. As we measure our own lives alongside his standard, we recognise these qualities not as vague aspirations, but as very real goals and targets for our own character and behaviour. It has often been noted that "fruit" is singular. The one fruit (Christ-likeness or holiness) is expressed in nine different ways. So we are not dealing with a situation like the rubric to an exam paper which might read, "Attempt any 4 questions". We do not select those which we think we might produce most easily and major on them. Nor do we add the individual qualities on to each other, one by one. They are all to be growing, all the time, if we are to become more like Christ.

However, while recognising the essential unity of the fruit, it is also helpful to group them in three groups of three. Love, joy and peace can be seen as the initial demonstration of the presence of the Holy Spirit in a new Christian's life. They are the signs of new birth, although they are never superseded. We never grow out of them, however long we may have been disciples of the Lord Jesus. Rather, we seek to grow into them, more and more. Because they are not abstract virtues, but evidences of Christ's life being in us, it follows that God is their only source and origin.

In a stimulating and helpful book, from a past generation, entitled "The Comforter", Montague Goodman traced this theme back to that other great passage of New Testament teaching on fruit-bearing in John 15. He pointed out that in the context of our Lord's address to his disciples in the upper room, he referred to the qualities of love, joy and peace as his own. In John 15:9 he exhorts them, "Remain in my love". Two verses later he says, "I have told you this so that my joy may be in you and that your joy may be complete." And in John 14:27, he had promised, "Peace I leave with you; my peace I give you.... Do not let your hearts be troubled and do not be afraid." All this underlines the fact that there is no other source apart from God himself. These characteristics can only come from God, and he imparts them to us, his people, as his Spirit produces his life within, as he "gets the job done". Such realities cannot be counterfeited. The world tries, of course, and sometimes we Christians try to generate them by our own efforts, but success of that sort depends on favourable circumstances. The Lord Jesus produces his fruit irrespective of the circumstances, and that is why it is fruit that lasts.

As we follow these themes through the New Testament, we discover that the fulness of the Spirit in the lives of his people means that each of these characteristics of the Lord Jesus can be experienced, to a superlative degree. On the theme of love, Paul prays that the Ephesian Christians may "know the love of Christ, which surpasses knowledge – that you may be filled with all the fulness of God" (Eph. 3:19) In addressing Christians who are facing great trials, Peter assures them that because they love the Lord Jesus and believe in him, they are "filled with an inexpressible and glorious joy" (1 Peter 1:8). Paul further promises those who consistently make their requests known to God, that "the peace of God which transcends all understanding will guard your hearts and your minds in Christ Jesus" (Phil. 4:7). It is significant that the dimensions in each case are extreme, in keeping with the fulness of the Holy Spirit. There is never any shortage of the divine resources.

Every new-born Christian knows something of these qualities, but the filled and fruitful Christian is increasing in each. If we return to John 15, we discover an important clue as to how this can happen. How are we to know Christ's love in us and remain in that love? In verse 10, the Lord Jesus tells us, "If you obey my commands, you will remain in my love". Obedience is the indispensable key. That is the bridge to verse 11, where he says, "I have told you this (about obedience) that my joy may be in you." How do we remain untroubled and unafraid in the midst of a threatening world? Jesus replies, "If anyone loves me, he will obey my teaching. My Father will love him, and we will come to him and make our home with him" (John 14:23). Again, obedience is the key – this time to peace. We respond to the Spirit's promptings as we do what Scripture tells us. We need deliberately and consciously to open every area of our lives as fully as we know, to the Lord. The more he fills, the more fruit we shall bear. As the life of the Spirit flows freshly into all our relationships, our thoughts, our attitudes and our motivation, the marks of his love, joy and peace will be seen increasingly in our words and actions. What we are inside is bound to become evident outside, as we live our lives in the world. When a cup that has been filled is jogged, whatever is inside spills over. So it is the knocks and reverses of life which demonstrate beyond dispute the quality of the life that is really within, whatever verbal claims to spirituality we may be wanting to make.

It is this outward dimension of life, with regard to our relationships with others, which seems to link together the next three qualities – patience, kindness and goodness. These are easier to see and estimate. Part of our development to maturity is that we are able to come to a sober assessment of ourselves and our true spiritual progress. Again, we have only to look to the Lord Jesus to see these virtues perfectly exemplified. Patience is sometimes translated as "long suffering". The example of Christ is seen in the way in which he endured such opposition from sinful men (Heb. 12:3). Yet not once did he retaliate or threaten (1 Peter 2:23). Instead he prayed for his persecutors, "Father forgive them, for they do not know what they are doing" (Luke 23:34). This quality may be described as living in the midst of a hostile world and yet feeling no hostility towards it. It is a love which suffers long, and that is only possible in a life which is controlled by the love of a God who "so loved the world that he gave his only Son". No human being can produce such love; it is the fruit of God's life alone.

The second quality of this trio, "kindness", may also be translated as graciousness or gentleness. The symbol of the Holy Spirit as a dove is particularly appropriate here. But sometimes we learn the positive qualities best by considering their opposite negatives. To me the most stark opposite is to consider how the leading politicians of rival parties speak of one another during an election campaign. The bitter hostility of rival factions is a prime symptom of our sinful human nature. We have an inbuilt tendency to destroy one another. It is the legacy of sin. Kindness, however, is the opposite pole. It is a child's word describing the adult who is prepared to make time to stop and listen, to enter his world and share his little anxieties and troubles which seem big enough to him. Children know the people who are kind to them. Since we know that quality of our heavenly Father too, we are to mirror it in our lives, in the way we speak of others, in the time and trouble we take with them, in the empathy we express for them, by actions, as well as in words.

The last of the second trio, "goodness", again takes us back to the Lord Jesus himself. He went about doing good, and the Gospels are full of the stories which illustrate this overflow of his love for people. There was a sense in which he could not help it, because it was the natural expression of his inner life. The fulness of the Holy Spirit will still produce goodness in our lives as we are moved by him to seize every opportunity to help others, to give time, energy or money, to bear burdens, encourage others and seek to build them up. This is not the busy-body "do-gooder" interfering in other people's lives for self-gratification, nor the cold duty that says "I do it because I ought to". This is the love that insists on doing all the good I can to all the people I can, by all the means I can. It is a revolutionary life-style, produced only by the Holy Spirit.

The last three qualities of the Spirit's fruit are inward, the focus being on our relationship with ourselves, although once again the evidence will always be able to be seen outwardly. The Holy Spirit still changes Christ's followers from the inside out, just as he did the original disciples. "Faithfulness" is the quality of internal dependability, which comes as the product of a life that is full of faith. It is seen outwardly in loyalty, reliability and an unwavering commitment. Again, this is not something that we have naturally, or can produce in our own strength. The disciples imagined it was, when Jesus warned them at the time of his passion that they would all fall away, and counselled them to watch and pray. They did not imagine it could really happen. They were not lacking in courage and resolve. Doubtless when Peter expressed his determination never to disown or leave Jesus, he really meant it, and many of his fellow disciples would have said the same. Yet the fact remains that when Jesus was arrested, in the Garden of Gethsemane, they all forsook him and fled. This makes the change in their behaviour in the book of Acts even more remarkable. In spite of the threats and punishments of the ruling authorities, those same disciples would not be silenced. "When they saw the courage of Peter and John and realised that they were unschooled, ordinary men, they were astonished and they took note that these men had been with Jesus" (Acts 5:29). What made the change? The answer is simple. The Holy Spirit, now living within them, was producing his fruit of faithfulness – to God and to his Word.

"Gentleness", or meekness, really has to do with teachability. Again, the contrast within the lives of the first disciples, before and after Pentecost, is remarkable and instructive. Several times in the gospels we find them jockeying for position, arguing about status and influence, wondering who would be the greatest, who would fill the key cabinet posts when the Lord set up his earthly kingdom. Their abrasive self-centredness is painfully obvious in the historical records. Clearly, it was something they later became very conscious of, because there is no attempt to exclude this strand from the gospel narratives, although one might have expected the apostles to want to suppress it, out of personal shame. But by that time, they were far too honest to do that. They had changed. You don't find that bluster and noise, with a stubborn insistence on getting their own way, in their behaviour in the book of Acts. They have their firm opinions about things and these sometimes clash, but overall there is a teachability and reasonableness about them in Acts, which is the gentleness, produced by the Spirit. Meekness is not weakness. It has nothing to do with indecision, or the unwillingness to assume proper responsibilities. It is the expression of a life dedicated to following in the footsteps of a servant king, who is meek and lowly of heart, gentle and humble (Matt. 11:29). It is the fruit of a life in which there is no longer any room for pride. That is the product of the Spirit within.

The last of the nine expressions of the Spirit's life is "self-control". Once more the Bible helps us to understand the meaning of the term, when we contrast the behaviour of the disciples before and after Pentecost. It was not for nothing that Jesus nicknamed James and John, "Boanerges", sons of thunder. Their desire to emulate Elijah in calling down fire from heaven on the villages that refused to receive them smacked more of pique than truly righteous indignation. Or, think of Peter's impetuosity, rushing into situations without pause for thought, over-reacting verbally and often in actions as well. But when the Spirit came, without dampening any of their zeal or enthusiasm, he brought a quality of measured, tempered control which made them different people. In Acts, the mind is in gear before the mouth is opened, and there is a sense of poise and confidence which even the hostile religious authorities were forced to recognise and marvel at. The Spirit's fruit is to bring every area of life under his controlling power. "Live by the Spirit and you will not gratify the desires of the sinful nature" (v. 16).

In fact, this concept of "desire" is foundational to Paul's teaching in this passage and to our understanding of the dynamic by which the fruit of the Spirit is increasingly produced in the life of the believer. From our earliest days we are aware of our own desires, some of which are perfectly natural and normal, such as those for food or sleep, but many of which are distorted by, or even produced from, the sinfulness of our fallen human nature. They are strong, reinforced by the world and the devil, and they clamour for gratification through self-indulgence (v. 16). But the Spirit also has desires, which are directly "contrary to the sinful nature" (v. 17), but which he is constantly promoting in the lives of God's people, as they are open and responsive to his promptings. This state of conflict is the normal experience of a Christian believer, with a redeemed but still fallen nature, living in a rebellious world.

Paul sums up the tension in our experience by the comment, "so you do not do what you want" (v. 17b). This clause clearly has a double edge to it. As we submit to the Spirit's desires and live in dependence on his power, we do not do what the sinful nature wants. But if we allow the fallen nature the upper hand by continuing to grieve the Spirit and by rejecting his gracious promptings, by choosing sin instead of God's grace, of course we shall not do what the redeemed nature, the new person that we have become in Christ, most deeply and truly desires. These deep desires for godliness of character, which the Spirit produces within us, generate the life-style described as the Spirit's fruit, in verses 22-23. It is a great encouragement to know that the will of the Spirit is involved in this ongoing process. We are not expected to do all the desiring ourselves; indeed, we cannot. God's sovereign will is active in accomplishing his desires, so that the production of his fruit in growing measure becomes as natural in the believer's life as apples are to an apple tree. It is all about the Holy Spirit being at the control-centre of our hearts and wills.

By contrast, when we read Paul's horrifying list of the acts of the sinful nature in verses 19-21, each one is evidence of a failure in the realm of self-control. The tragedy of sin is the slavery it always brings, because its victims are taken over by uncontrollable desires and passion. But the miracle of regeneration is that when we are in Christ, our lives are under the Spirit's supervision and control, which brings a dignity to life that is the true hallmark of what it means to be a human being, created in the image of God. There will always be a battle (v. 17), but through Christ's victory on the cross, evidenced by the empty tomb and his ascension to glory, we have been given the greatest resource we could ever receive, in order to win through – the life of God in the soul of man, through the indwelling Holy Spirit. All that is necessary has been done. The divine resources are available for every believer, every moment of every day. "Those who belong to Christ Jesus have crucified the sinful nature with its passions and desires. Since we live by the Spirit, let us keep in step with the Spirit" (vv. 24-25).

It is striking that the great event referred to in the past tense here is the foundation on which our present experience is built and the means by which it is developed. So, the crucifixion of our sinful nature (v. 24) has already happened. Paul is not exhorting his readers to bring it about. It is the given, objective reality of the Christian life. When we first come to Christ our old self-centred rebellious way of living is nailed to the cross, in a definitive way, as we turn from sin, in true repentance. That is the essential objective change which has taken place at conversion, which deals with our sin and fallenness and makes it possible for us to live the new life of the Spirit. Again, it is assumed that this is the norm for all Christians ("since we live by the Spirit" v. 25). We do not have to bring it about. It is the miracle of regeneration, which is God's work alone. Our part is to "keep in step with the Spirit", to keep pace with his desires, to respond to his directions and to embrace his priorities. It will then be the most (super)natural thing for him increasingly, to produce his fruit, in our lives.

6.

RECEIVING THE SPIRIT'S GIFTS

1 CORINTHIANS 12:1-11

Now about spiritual gifts, brothers, I do not want you to be ignorant. You know that when you were pagans, somehow or other you were influenced and led astray to dumb idols. Therefore I tell you that no-one who is speaking by the Spirit of God says, "Jesus be cursed", and no-one can say, "Jesus is Lord", except by the Holy Spirit. There are different kinds of gifts, but the same Spirit. There are different kinds of service but the same Lord. There are different kinds of working, but the same God works all of them in all men. Now to each one the manifestation of the Spirit is given for the common good. To one there is given through the Spirit the message of wisdom, to another the message of knowledge by means of the same Spirit, to another faith by the same Spirit, to another gifts of healing by that one Spirit, to another miraculous powers, to another prophecy, to another the ability to distinguish between spirits, to another the ability to speak in different kinds of tongues, and to still another the interpretation of tongues. All these are the work of one and the same Spirit, and he gives them to each one, just as he determines." (1 Cor. 12:1-11)

No series of studies on the Holy Spirit could possibly be complete without some consideration of the gifts of the Spirit, which have sadly been the occasion of so much strife and division among Christians, in recent years. The same situation had arisen in the church at Corinth and it is therefore one of the major areas of concern addressed by Paul in his first letter. Before we look at the text of chapter 12, it will be important to realise something about the context in which it occurs. Chapters 12-14 constitute a major unit in the book as a whole. Paul has already been dealing at some length with the doctrinal and moral pressures the church was facing, both from rival teachers, who proclaimed a different gospel, and from the secular culture.

Now, he turns to the church at Corinth in terms of its own internal life and work, demonstrated in its corporate worship and service. Here the question he tackles concerns the nature of Christian authority. Paul had faced a good deal of personal opposition within the congregation which he had founded. Some were refusing to endorse his ministry on the grounds that he failed to meet up to the standards of rhetorical excellence, which were derived from the travelling philosophers of the day. He was neither eloquent, nor intellectually impressive enough. In reply, Paul shows how this raises the larger and more important question of what criteria are to be used to distinguish the spurious from the real in the church's work and worship? Are spiritual gifts the main evidence of genuine spiritual life, or are other considerations a more reliable guide? Should those who seem to demonstrate the most remarkable gifts be given the greatest authority in the church?

There is no doubt that we are dealing with a distinct unit in chapters 12-14. The heading is clearly spelt out in verse 1, although the word "gifts" does not occur in the Greek text. Literally, it reads "about spirituals". Gifts were a major issue at Corinth, but these chapters take us beyond the outward manifestations to the inner life, which is always the primary focus of interest in Scripture. It is the whole range of spiritual matters within the church which is engaging Paul's attention. Clearly, there were problems of spiritual pride at Corinth. Those who had the more noticeable public gifts tended to parade them, with the result that others without these gifts were tempted either to feel unimportant, or to become jealous. Chapter 12 begins by seeking to correct that wrong attitude. There can be no room for pride, because every ministry is a gift from God. They are not marks of an individual's worthiness, but gifts of God's grace. There can be no room for grumbling or jealousy then, just because these are God's decisions. Each believer has some kind of gift (v. 7), every gift is needed (v. 7) and it is God who decides sovereignly on their distribution (v. 11). No member of Christ's body is unimportant to the well-being of the whole.

But Paul doesn't stop there. He does not want his readers to be fatalistic about this matter of God's sovereignty. So, after expounding the picture of the church as a body (12:12-30), he exhorts them eagerly to desire the greater gifts (v. 31). Yet even the greatest gifts can be exercised in an unspiritual way, so chapter 13 expounds to us "the most excellent way" which is using the gifts in love. Then in chapter 14, which expounds on that theme, the practical outworking of love is shown to mean subjecting every exercise or manifestation of spiritual gifts to the one end, that the church may be built up in Christ. The measure of the greatness of any particular gift is neither its degree of impressiveness, nor its apparent miraculous nature, but its usefulness to the church. That is why the gifts regarding the ministry of the Word are identified as of major importance (12:28a). Quite simply, they build the church up most. With these general markers in position, we can now focus on our passage in more detail.

THE PROOF OF REALITY (VV. 1-3)

The overall purpose of Scripture is always to expel our ignorance of God and his ways through the revelation of his character and will, which is absolute truth. When the mind is enlightened, then the will can be energised and the whole life will be changed in increasing conformity to the will of God. Paul seems to be indicating in these verses that there was a considerable degree of ignorance and inexperience in what was going on in the church at Corinth. We should not forget that the immediately preceding chapters have been dealing at some length with the issue of idolatry. Apparently, there were many former idolaters in the church, who had not yet broken completely with their pagan customs. Some had only a marginal understanding of the demands and implications of their new faith. People who claimed to be directly inspired by God seem to have been coming to the times of congregational worship in order to give what amounted to a very impressive performance in their use of spiritual gifts. Similar phenomena would be familiar to them from the days of their pagan worship festivals. They prophesied with great emotion and fervour, but at times they were so "carried away" that they seem to have said some very disturbing things, even blaspheming Christ and calling him "anathema" (cursed) as verse 3 indicates.

Naturally, the question arose as to whether the Holy Spirit was empowering them, at least in the light of such extreme utterances. Could the church trust any, all or none of the messages which these people passed on? And if not, was their exercise of any other "gifts" to be accepted as valid? . That is the situation which Paul is addressing here. Verse 3 begins with the linking word "therefore", because he does not want them to be ignorant about spiritual gifts (v. 1) and because their lives previous to their conversion would have included attendance at the temples of dumb idols (v. 2). These idols could not speak. Their only 'messengers' or 'prophets' were under the influence of demonic inspiration. Clearly, these young Corinthian believers had very little godly spiritual experience on which to draw, when trying to decide whether or not so-called "inspired" speech was actually under the influence of the Holy Spirit. Since spiritual things have to be spiritually discerned (1 Cor. 2:14) even a study of comparative religious phenomena would have been quite inadequate to the task.

So, what method can be used to test for reality? Verse 3 provides the litmus paper, but it goes further than simply providing a test for false prophets. That would be to read the verse in too simplistic a way. We are not looking at the simple repetition of what might be regarded as an almost magic formula – "Jesus is Lord". That would not necessarily help discernment at all. For a false prophet could be very careful never to say "Jesus be cursed" and he might well affirm and agree verbally that "Jesus is Lord" precisely to gain acceptance with the church. Similarly, there might be a genuine Christian who could say "Jesus is Lord" from the heart, but whose so-called "prophecy" lacked any real empowering of the Holy Spirit. Genuine spiritual ministry is not merely a matter of repeating a formula. The words must represent the speaker's own life and conviction. In all normal circumstances, blasphemy indicates unbelief, while the fundamental confession of Christ's lordship indicates the existence of saving faith. The words spoken indicate the presence or absence of the Holy Spirit in the life of the speaker. And since you cannot be a Christian without the indwelling of the Spirit, this can be used as a test of genuine Christian faith.

In verse 3, Paul is teaching us that conversion is a sovereign work of God, and not of man. Only true believers can possess the spiritual gifts which will benefit the church, because only they are indwelt by the Holy Spirit, who is the giver. Paul's argument is that "Jesus is Lord" is a personal confession. The speaker is speaking out of his heart, so that the words he speaks are his own, chosen by him. The phrase speaking "by the Spirit" does not mean that the Holy Spirit speaks the words for him, as though he was totally dominated by the Spirit, in a state of ecstasy. The speaker here is not saying "This is what the Holy Spirit says", but "This is what I say because the Holy Spirit has enlightened me". This of itself provides an important insight into the nature of New Testament prophecy, which is seen to be rational and controlled, rather than unpredictable and ecstatic. "The spirits of the prophets are subject to the control of prophets", as Paul states at the end of the section, in 14:32.

Amid the many claims and counter-claims which abound in these areas today, we owe it to ourselves to ensure that we have grasped this vital Biblical principle and that we are not easily deluded by ignorance. The lordship of Christ is the ultimate proof of spiritual reality. And that must be both confessed in words and demonstrated in life. If those essential ingredients are absent then we have every right to question whether the expression of any spiritual phenomena has its origins with the Holy Spirit, or is really Christian at all. We are not to be impressed by noise and enthusiasms, but by likeness to Christ. That is always the hallmark of the Spirit's work, so that whenever submission to Christ as Lord is absent (as for example in a refusal to submit to the authority of Scripture as his inspired Word), there is no indication that what is being exercised is a gift of the Spirit. It is more likely to be a manifestation of the energy of the flesh.

THE PRIORITY OF UNITY (VV. 4-6)

This essential characteristic of the people of God is grounded in the Trinity itself. Because God is one, in three persons, his body on earth is to be one. Within the holy Trinity, this unity is represented by each person of the Godhead playing a unique role. It is a particular work of the Holy Spirit to bear witness to the lordship of Jesus. Indeed, that is his great task and delight. Only the Spirit can do this and any claimed inspiration which does not bear his hallmark does not come from him. In these verses, the theme of diversity in unity is the focus of Paul's argument, but the priority is unity. So there is the one Spirit (v. 4) who is both Lord (v. 5) and God (v. 6) – surely a Trinitarian reference. In his gracious plans and purposes, he uses a variety of ways and means to bring human beings under the lordship of Christ, for that is his supreme goal.

Paul divides the Spirit's operations into three categories. The first are different kinds of gifts of grace (v. 4) – the word is "charismata", signifying that they are freely and generously given. Different gifts are distributed to different individuals. All Christians do not receive the same gift, or gifts, but all the gifts come from the one Spirit. No one has all of the gifts, nor should have; but every Christian has at least one, for every Christian has the Spirit (Rom. 8:9).

Paul's second reference is to "ministries", by which he means to indicate different ways of serving (v. 5). The important thing to remember here is that it is not status, but function, which he has in view. All true service must be offered under Christ's lordship, and in the power of his indwelling life. The kinds of service will vary, but they are all for the Lord and in the Lord. This ensures that together they build the unity of Christ's body, although such acts of service may require no special "gift".

The third category, "works" or "workings", could also be translated activities (v. 6). Here it is the thought of God's power or energy in action which is uppermost. The stress falls on the same God who is active in all of his people, which puts the emphasis on unity. This brings us to a momentous principle, namely that wherever gifts for ministries cause divisions between Christians, the way they are being used is actually denying God's purposes in giving them to the church. At base, we must accept one another and our differences of gifting as God-given. Members of a church will differ in temperament, social background and experience, but also in gifts. We should learn to praise God for that, and not expect uniformity of experience or service.

We have no right to put other Christians through our own particular hoops, to demand that they have our special experiences, or do things our way. Unity is found in the Spirit who gives, the Lord who is served, and the God who is at work. All that we have and are comes from him, and he works in and through us all, so that we are all valued and all needed. We must not expect one person to have an impossible accumulation of gifts and then criticise him for what he lacks. Nor should we become discontented with ourselves if we have not received a particular gift which we think we would like to have. Rather, we must start thanking God for what we do have and using the gifts he has given us, in the fellowship of his church, for his glory. What God joins together we dare not divide or separate. That is a vital Biblical principle.

THE PURPOSE IN DIVERSITY (vv. 7-11)

There are nine gifts listed in verses 8-10, but the two verses on either side are the most important ingredients of the teaching to grasp in this section. Firstly, let us look at the diversity of gifts. Clearly, this is not an exhaustive list. Others are found in Ephesians 4:11 and Romans 12:6-8. There is no word here to indicate that all of these have to appear either in every church, or in every generation. The Holy Spirit is the sovereign giver.

However, in common with all the other lists in the New Testament, it is the Word gifts which come first and are given the greatest priority. The messages of wisdom and knowledge are clearly very closely related. They have to do with understanding the mind and plan of God (see 1 Cor. 2:6-10) and communicating this revelation to others. Some have identified wisdom as being more practical and pastoral, whereas knowledge may be more reflective and theological. But we have to recognise that no-one can be entirely sure of their precise terms of reference, in the Corinthian context, which should be a warning to us not to jump to the conclusion that manifestations which are claimed to be the same gifts in action today are necessarily so. They might well have been teaching gifts in the understanding and application of Scripture, rather than implying any direct form of supernatural revelation.

In verse 9, the focus is more on the will, rather than the mind. There is a special gift of faith, given to some believers in order to equip them to accomplish otherwise impossible tasks. In terms of Biblical examples, we can think of Noah's almost superhuman task in building the ark, Abraham's summons to leave the security of Ur for an unknown land at the age of seventy, or Elijah's lonely stand against the hundreds of prophets of Baal on Mount Carmel. In later generations, we can think of William Carey, George Müller, Gladys Aylward or Corrie ten Boom. Doubtless, there are many unsung heroes of faith in our own generation, who are gifted by God to believe his word against all the odds and to fulfil his purposes in quite remarkable ways, to believe great things from God and attempt great things for him.

That sort of faith may well be related to the "gifts of healings" and "miraculous powers", referred to in verses 9 and 10. The plural is surely significant here, indicating not a gift of healing to be exercised indiscriminately through one person who has the touch, but actual cases of healing carried out by God, through a human agent, probably through prayer and the laying on of hands, as taught and exemplified in James 5:14. A Biblical example of miraculous powers as a special gift of God may be when Paul inflicted blindness on Elymas, the sorcerer, at Paphos (Acts 13:11). Whatever the disagreements and debates that rage around these matters in the contemporary church, no Christian should ever want to limit, much less deny, the power of God when he chooses to work, through whatever means he sovereignly selects. Every believing praying church has seen God's power at work in healing the sick, sometimes through, and sometimes without, medical means. We know that God's power is not diminished one iota and that through his Spirit he is still as active as ever in his world. But we do not bring glory to God by accepting uncritically all the contemporary claims to healing, which are frequently made, but rarely substantiated. God does not need to "construct" healings, in order to give his gospel credibility. In fact some of the "hype" that is associated with the extreme fringes of the healing movement sadly seems to create the opposite effect in the unbelieving world.

Perhaps one important corrective here, which should be understood and applied far more than it commonly is, lies in the Bible's emphasis on the nature of the gift, rather than the channel of its use. All of these "charismata" issue from God, in their origin and application, and "are the work of one and the same Spirit" (v. 11a). The human agencies through whom they are manifested are entirely subsidiary. God does not need any of us to accomplish his work, but he graciously catches us up in his purposes and gives us the immense privilege of being involved in his activity "just as he determines" (v. 11b). It is a mark of our fallen self-centredness and our persistent tendency to rebellious independence that we delight perversely to focus on the human agent rather than the divine giver. So, we elevate prophets and preachers, healers and miracle workers, as though they were the originators of the gifts. We want to put them on a pedestal and, quite frankly, many of them are only too happy to let us. That is how the envy and jealousy, or the sense of inferiority and inadequacy which Paul goes on to deal with in verses 14-26 come about. The fact of the matter is that the channel is completely unimportant.

I take this to mean also that there is no automatic guarantee that a gift once exercised will always be experienced or "available" through a particular individual. Our gifts are not necessarily given permanently or irrevocably, unlike our salvation. God may choose to use any of his people in any way at any time. If we relate this to the extended list of gifts at the end of the chapter, in verses 28-30, where helping others and gifts of administration are included, it becomes clear that while no one believer will demonstrate all the gifts, the glory of the church is that different Christians are equipped by God to accomplish his work, in a huge variety of ways, and they all have their own particular part to play. As has often been said, the glory goes not to the donkey but to the King who rides on its back; not to the Christian servant, however "gifted" he or she may be thought to be, but to the Christ who reigns.

The last four gifts listed here relate to what goes on in the congregational gatherings of God's people. There are differing views as to what the precise meaning of "prophecy" was in Corinth and how it should relate to us today, nearly two thousand years on, when God's written revelation has been complete for so many centuries. But what is clear is that the gift involves speaking the authoritative Word of God, with powerful directness and unmistakable relevance to the hearers. Such human words are not in themselves infallible. They have to be discerned and tested against the plumb-line of the known Word of God, already given in the Scriptures. The fact that a Christian brother claims to be speaking a word from the Lord is not in itself sufficient guarantee that it is indeed so.

The Reformers' emphasis on the right of private judgment, based on their belief in the perspicuity of Scripture, is important here. Every believer is promised the Holy Spirit's illumination of the Word of truth, when that is humbly sought. The Scriptures are themselves clear in all their major teachings (though there will always be passages we find difficult to understand) so that they are not the preserve of a professional elite, but the birth-right of every true Christian. Each of us, therefore, has the responsibility of judging what we hear by the known word, which God has already spoken. As Paul instructed the Thessalonians, "Do not treat prophecies with contempt. Test everything. Hold on to the good" (1 Thess. 5:20-21).

The same checks and safeguards are advocated with regard to the gift of tongues. Without interpretation, which is also a gift, there can be no edification of the hearers. Again, the manifestation of the phenomenon is not in itself a guarantee of the Spirit's activity, since tongues exist in non-Christian religious manifestations as well. Paul is almost certainly correcting an over-emphasis on the gift within the church at Corinth, by deliberately putting it at the end of his list.

To discuss the nature of these "charismata" in detail and to explore the intricacies of the debates which have developed around their continuing existence and significance is beyond the purpose of this chapter. Such a discussion would require a book in itself and, of course, many have been written from a variety of standpoints. My intention here has been to identify the essential principles which the apostle Paul was so concerned to stress, and I will try to summarise these in the last paragraph of this chapter. But overarching the whole discussion is the affirmation of the lordship of Jesus Christ, with which the section began (v. 3).

When we ask how his lordship is mediated to his people today, the Bible is unequivocal about its answer, that it is by his Spirit, through his Word. That principle has not changed since the New Testament was first written. Jesus himself indissolubly linked his authority to his Word. "Heaven and earth will pass away, but my words will never pass away" (Mark 13:31). Nor is this just an intellectual acceptance of his teaching or a theological position about his person. "Not everyone who says to me, 'Lord, Lord', will enter the kingdom of heaven but only he who does the will of my Father who is in heaven " (Matt 7:21). And how can we ever know that will, unless it is articulated in the word that the Father has spoken, in Christ? This is also the Spirit's great work of revelation. "The Spirit gives life; the flesh counts for nothing. The words I have spoken to you are spirit and they are life" (John 6:63). So, Jesus binds together the authority of his words and the life-giving power of his Spirit and they are never to be separated.

The clear inference from this is that all contemporary claims to be speaking on behalf of the Lord must be evaluated, with regard to their content, by all that we know the Lord has already said, unchangingly and with total authority in the sixty-six books of canonical Scripture. That is what it means to live under the lordship of Christ, in this area. Whatever claims may be made for a contemporary gift of prophecy, no Christian who is committed to the authority of Christ and the sufficiency of Scripture will claim that what is being "revealed" should be written down and bound into the Bible, as a sixty-seventh book. There are people who claim such inspiration, of course, but as soon as their words are given an authority equivalent to that of Scripture, the Bible is increasingly closed and ignored, and the exciting, urgent word of the prophet begins to take over. This is how the sub-Christian cults and sects have almost always begun, often with eventually devastatingly destructive results. Such "adding" to Scripture will inevitably subtract from Christ and his words, since they are now considered insufficient, and so subtly undermine his lordship in the lives of those who receive them.

But what about lesser examples, when a sincere Christian believes that God has given them "a word" to pass on to another individual or congregation? Again, the fact that the claim is made, "I have a word from the Lord for you", is no guarantee that it is so. The Bible has frequent warnings about the self-delusion of false prophets and their ability to lead others astray, even with great enthusiasm and conviction. Everything must be tested by what God has already said. If the "word" given is in accordance with Scripture, then it may be an encouragement to go on believing that truth, which seems innocuous enough. But it would be much more helpful if it was given directly from Scripture itself, so that as the hearer I would be encouraged to go on putting my faith in the Word of God and not the words of a man.

Many preachers' stories are told about Charles Haddon Spurgeon, the great nineteenth century Baptist pastor, in London. Probably, most of them are apocryphal, but on one occasion Spurgeon is supposed to have been approached by a woman at the end of a preaching service, who confided that she had a word from the Lord for him. After refusing for a while to receive it, eventually Spurgeon succumbed and was told, "Your name is written in the Lamb's book of life". To this he replied that he wished she had not said this, because before, he was trusting for his assurance in the word of Christ alone, but now she was tempting him to put his trust in the word of a mere human being. Such "messages" are not perhaps as innocuous as they sometimes seem.

Or what about guidance messages for individuals or for congregations? "The Lord has told me that we should rebuild the church hall" would be one such example. Is this authoritative prophecy? If the Lord really has told the speaker then this word must be obeyed, but many equally sincere believers within congregations may say, "The Lord has not told me!" This sort of "prophecy" is often so divisive that one must question whether its origin can possibly be with the Spirit of truth, who is the author of unity. It may be sincerely given, but at the same time be highly manipulative. Why would God give such a message to one individual, when he has given his Spirit in abundant measure to every true believer, within that congregation? Such messages may have been divinely given on occasions in the Old Testament period, but this was before the gift of the Spirit to all who believe in Christ. The Urim and the Thummim (Deut 33:8, Num 27:21) and the casting of lots were other ways God authorised for the discovery of his will in Israel. But now Christ has come and following the cross and resurrection, the Spirit has been given to all his believing people (John 7:37-39, Acts 2:38-39). We are no longer in need of prophets to be channels of God's mind, for we have the fully sufficient Scriptures, the revelatory ministry of the Spirit and the mind of Christ (1 Cor. 2:9-16).

The elders and pastors of every congregation have the responsibility of weighing any claim to be God speaking, which is external to the word of Scripture, including preaching, and especially when it is not expository. We dare not allow what Paul describes as "savage wolves" to come among God's flock, or even to come from among our own number "and distort the truth in order to draw away disciples after them" (Acts 20:29-30). Even though they seem to be quite harmless, appearing at first as rather woolly sheep, the stakes are far too high to allow any and every notion to be peddled as the word of God. Such claims should never be glibly accepted and that is even more the case when they are soothing words which our "itching ears" want to hear. We are all too readily turned away from sound teaching to our own desires, to the myths and fantasies of "a great number of teachers", as Paul warned the Ephesians of his day in his letter to their pastor, Timothy (2 Tim. 4:3-4). No excitement about prophecy must be permitted to divert us from obedience to the Lord Jesus, whose will was mediated through his Spirit-inspired apostle, when he gave this solemn charge to Timothy, "Preach the Word; be prepared in season and out of season; correct, rebuke and encourage – with great patience and careful instruction" (2 Tim. 4:1-2). Nothing must undermine that great gift of the Spirit. Nothing must subvert the lordship of Christ, mediated through the infallible and inerrant word of Scripture.

As we close this chapter, we need to return to the themes of verse 7. These manifestations of the Spirit are given "for the common good". Spiritual gifts are not distributed to satisfy our personal spiritual appetite or greed, much less to bolster up our self-image and pride. They are for serving the Lord, by building up his body. Each Christian has a responsibility before God, to use whatever gifts he or she may have to increase the body's strength and promote its unity. That is why they have been given in the sovereign will of God. We cannot dictate the gifts which we, or others, should have. It is God alone who chooses (v. 11). His gifts suit both the needs and capacities of every individual member of Christ's body, through whom they are exercised, as well as ministering to the needs of the body as a whole. So there must be no rivalry or division over these things, but harmony and mutual acceptance. Then we shall be living in such a way as to demonstrate that Jesus truly is Lord.

7.

LOVE
- THE SPIRIT'S LIFE-STYLE

1 CORINTHIANS 12:27-14:1

Now you are the body of Christ, and each one of you is a part of it. And in the church God has appointed first of all apostles, second prophets, third teachers, then workers of miracles, also those having gifts of healing, those able to help others, those with gifts of administration, and those speaking in different kinds of tongues. Are all apostles? Are all prophets? Are all teachers? Do all work miracles? Do all have gifts of healing? Do all speak in tongues? Do all interpret? But eagerly desire the greater gifts. And now I will show you the most excellent way. If I speak in tongues of men and of angels, but have not love, I am only a resounding gong or a clanging cymbal. If I have the gift of prophecy and can fathom all mysteries and all knowledge, and if I have a faith that can move mountains, but have not love, I am nothing. If I give all I possess to the poor and surrender my body to the flames, but have not love, I gain nothing. Love is patient, love is kind. It does not envy, it does not boast, it is not proud. It is not rude, it is not self-seeking, it is not easily angered, it keeps no record of wrongs. Love does not delight in evil but rejoices with the truth. It always protects, always trusts, always hopes, always perseveres. Love never fails. But where there are prophecies, they will cease; where there are tongues, they will be stilled; where there is knowledge, it will pass away. For we know in part and we prophesy in part, but when perfection comes, the imperfect disappears. When I was a child, I talked like a child, I thought like a child, I reasoned like a child. When I became a man, I put childish ways behind me. Now we see but a poor reflection as in a mirror; then we shall see face to face. Now I know in part; then I shall know fully, even as I am fully known. And now these three remain: faith hope and love. But the greatest of these is love. Follow the way of love and eagerly desire spiritual gifts, especially the gift of prophecy. (1 Cor. 12:27-14:1)

The New Testament uses a number of vivid pictures to define and describe the nature of the church. We are the flock of God (dependent, but protected and provided for) and Christ is the shepherd. We are the bride of Christ and he is the husband, nurturing and caring for his people in an intimate relationship of love. We are the body of Christ and he is the head. This is a metaphor of inter-dependence, of diversity within unity, of working together with one purpose under the direction of the Lord. To be a Christian means, by definition, to be united to Christ, by faith. It follows, then, that in the one body of Christ, which is the universal church, we are inter-dependent members of one another. Spiritual "lone-rangers" are a contradiction in terms.

Earlier in 1 Corinthians 12, immediately following on from his treatment of the spiritual gifts, which we explored in the last chapter, Paul has been at pains to stress the ministry of the Spirit in our corporate experience of life within the church. He uses the human body as an analogy. It is a single unit, an organism, which lives and grows through a wide variety of functions, in which many separate parts of the body have to perform their own unique role, but in harmony. One has only to think of the complexity of the process of eating and digesting food with so many different parts of the body involved to see how suitable an illustration it is. The oneness comes from the obedience of each part to the central control. "So it is with Christ," Paul continues "for we were all baptised by one Spirit into one body – whether Jews or Greeks, slave or free – and we were all given the one Spirit to drink." (1 Cor. 12:13) It is the Spirit's function to unite together all of Christ's faithful people, since he is the same life flowing through each one, from the head. As Goodspeed translates the verse, "We have all been saturated with the Spirit". That is what unites Christians.

How unspeakably tragic it was (and is!) that such believers should make the Spirit's ministry, gifts or graces the cause of division, even schism in the body! If the same Spirit permeates every believer, then racial differences or social status no longer have any significance. And if these worldly distinctives are irrelevant in the church of Christ, we must be very careful indeed not to raise other alternative barriers of so-called superior gifts, experiences or spirituality, in their place. Such distinctions may appear to have a thin veneer of Christian authenticity, but actually in New Testament terms they indicate a pseudo-spirituality.

The rest of chapter 12 is devoted to dealing with the outcome of the false divisions in the Corinthian church, as they had affected the ordinary members. Some were saying that they did not matter because their gifts seemed inferior; they felt they did not belong. They looked at the impressive performances of the gifted members of their congregation and deduced that, because they could never compete, they did not count. Paul's answer (1 Cor. 12:17) is to show that no member can fulfil another's ministry. The foot and ear may not be able to perform the complicated functions of the hand or eye, but who would want to be without them? They are to stop thinking of themselves as inferior if they are not in the limelight. Who is to say that those with a hidden ministry of prayer are not actually far more important to the church than its public, up-front leaders?

Equivalently, on the other side, some members of the Corinthian church were clearly suffering from a superiority complex that was only too ready to turn on others and convey the message, "We don't need you". Paul's treatment (1 Cor. 12:21-26) is to remind them that even if one member of the body fulfils his own role superbly well, he still depends on the supporting work of every other member. When we start to compare ourselves with other Christians, it usually leads either to jealousy and discouragement, or to pride and complacency. Either set of attitudes injures the body, and both are wrong, because we are not to judge one another, or ourselves, against the criteria of what others do. The only valid assessment is on the grounds of faithfulness to God in developing whatever gifts he has sovereignly chosen to give us. There should be "equal concern for each other" (v. 25b) since the healthy function of every individual part is vital for the whole. If one part is in pain, the rest cannot be at peace. The unity of the Spirit means that we feel for one another, sharing each other's suffering and rejoicing in one another's honours.

In the year AD 257, the Roman Emperor Valerian ordered the confiscation of the church's treasures throughout the empire, as part of his general move against Christians and to augment the imperial coffers, no doubt. The story is told of a deacon called Lawrence who was confronted by the emperor's messengers, determined to enforce his adherence to Valerian's edict. "Where are the church's treasures?" they demanded. In reply, the deacon flung open the church doors, to reveal the sanctuary crowded with the poor, the sick and the handicapped. "Here are the church's treasures", he exclaimed. As much as the Corinthians, we need the reminder of the infinite value attributed by God to every one of his people, every member of Christ's body. "Now you are the body of Christ, and each one of you is a part of it". (1 Cor. 12:27)

It is against this background that we come to the thirteenth chapter, possibly the most well-known, but most frequently misunderstood chapter in the whole of the New Testament. But how much deeper we find its significance to be when we see it in context, not as a lofty panegyric on the theme of love, but as a down-to-earth exposition of the Spirit's life-style. Immediately preceding the chapter, Paul has exhorted the church eagerly to desire the greater gifts (1 Cor. 12:31). In chapter 14 he will explain that the criterion of "greatness" is not impressive performance or noisy self-promotion, but how much other Christians are built up by them. The edification of the church is the purpose of the 'charismata'. However, there is something even better than seeking the greater gifts, which Paul describes as "the most excellent way", and that is using whatever gifts we have, in love.

LOVE ALONE COUNTS (VV. 1-3)

There is a progression in these verses through the gifts and activities of Christian service, from the lesser to the greatest, from tongues (v. 1) to martyrdom (v. 3). But the same lesson is being driven home each time. Only love gives value to the exercise of any of the spiritual gifts. When Paul speaks of "the tongues of men and of angels", many have followed Calvin's view that this means both human languages miraculously given as on the day of Pentecost, and also ecstatic speech as was being practised at Corinth, which may have had no discernible linguistic structure or shape. Others suggest it could be simply the expression of a superlative – "No matter how wonderfully developed my use of tongues may be..." Either way, without love in the speaker expressed by the use of the gift, its exercise is hollow, like the hollow noise of a gong or cymbal. These two instruments were widely used in pagan temples to call the god's attention, or to drive away evil spirits. Loveless use of tongues is not only empty, it is no better than pagan. Just as the Old Testament prophets denounced outward worship which was not accompanied by heart-obedience, so Paul denounces gifts without love as meaningless noise.

We need to note that it is only the Spirit who can make the difference. The problem throughout the Old Testament was that the covenant demands were never more than external. Written on tablets of stone, they presented a standard which the sinful nature of even the most devoted Israelite precluded him from fulfilling. So there was always a looking forward, to a deeper relationship, a more personal knowledge of God, a better day. In Jeremiah's famous words, "'This is the covenant that I will make with the house of Israel after that time' declares the LORD. 'I will put my law in their minds and write it on their hearts. I will be their God, and they will be my people. No longer will a man teach his neighbour, or a man his brother, saying, 'Know the LORD,' because they will all know me from the least of them to the greatest,' declares the LORD." (Jer 31:33-34). The same predictive confidence rings out in Ezekiel's words "This is what the Sovereign LORD says, ... 'I will take you out of the nations ... I will gather you ... I will cleanse you ... I will give you a new heart and put a new spirit in you; I will remove from you your heart of stone and give you a heart of flesh. And I will put my Spirit in you and move you to follow my decrees'.." (Ezek. 36:22-27). Only the Spirit can internalise God's truth and write it "not with ink but with the Spirit of the living God, not on tablets of stone but on tablets of human hearts" (2 Cor. 3:3).

This is precisely the miracle of the new covenant. Although the Spirit was, of course, active throughout the period of the old covenant, there are certain qualitative differences. Under the old covenant, the Spirit came upon certain selected individuals, not the whole community, to equip them for particular forms of ministry. In Exodus 31:2ff, God says that he has chosen Bezalel "and I have filled him with the Spirit of God, with skill, ability and knowledge in all kinds of crafts – to make artistic designs for work in gold, silver and bronze, to cut and set stones, to work in wood, and to engage in all kinds of craftsmanship." But the Spirit might equally leave those whom he had empowered. After Samuel anointed David to be king, before Saul was removed from the throne, we read that "from that day on the Spirit of the LORD came upon David in power" (1 Sam. 16:13). The immediate result was his victory over Goliath, as the Lord's anointed, in a situation where Saul and the armies of Israel had been paralysed by fear. But after David's adultery with Bathsheba and the murder of Uriah, we find him pleading with God, in his penitential prayer, "Do not take your Holy Spirit from me" (Ps. 51:11). It was a very real possibility for even the most godly were not permanently indwelt by the Spirit in the Old Testament period.

The point is further made in the teaching of Jesus, together with the evangelist's explanation, in John's Gospel, chapter 7, verses 37-39. On the last day of the Feast of Tabernacles, when for a week the pilgrims had seen water poured out daily as a memorial of God's provision for his people in the wilderness, Jesus made an astounding claim. In a loud voice, he declared, "If a man is thirsty let him come to me and drink." He was claiming to be able to satisfy the deepest human needs, that by believing in him anyone might have access to "streams of living water from within". It is of course effectively a claim to be God. And John adds this explanation. "By this he meant the Spirit, whom those who believed in him were later to receive. Up to that time the Spirit had not been given, since Jesus had not yet been glorified." A study of John's Gospel reveals that the glorification of Jesus is his "lifting up" on the cross. In other words, the gift of the Spirit is the fruit of Christ's passion and exaltation. Calvary had to come before Pentecost. Pardon always precedes power. It was the ascended Christ, the victor of the cross and the empty tomb, who apportioned his grace and gave gifts to men (Eph. 4:7-8), the greatest of which is his Spirit, through whom all other gifts and graces flow.

So, when Paul tells the Corinthian church that spiritual gifts exercised without Christian love are a contradiction in terms, this is not just a narrow opinion designed to deal with a local incident. The whole purpose and privilege of New Covenant Christianity is at stake. Only the indwelling Spirit can create the love which is the mark of authentic Christ-likeness.

Back in 1 Corinthians 13, at verse 2, Paul moves up the scale of gifts to prophecy. Again, he imagines its development to a superlative degree. Suppose one "can fathom all mysteries and all knowledge." Without love, it is all one big zero. It would be to speak God's word without God's tone of voice. Truth without love ceases to be fully truth. Miracle-working faith is brought under the same assessment. Moving mountains means the seemingly impossible happening. But even more startling is Paul's assertion that amazing things could happen from entirely wrong motives. If it is personal kudos, fame, applause or any human glory that motivates, rather than love, in God's eyes it is worth nothing.

Finally, the apostle considers even martyrdom. I can divide my property up into fragments to share it with as many people as possible, but it can be heartless and loveless. Even giving can be motivated by the recognition of others or the acquisition of merit. Without love, nothing is gained. Not even the ultimate gift of one's own life is exempt from that judgment. The body may be surrendered to the flames, but God's concern is with the heart. All of these actions could conceivably be motivated by self-love, rather than the self-giving, which is the root of true love. But without such love, on heaven's balance sheet they come to nothing. Only love counts with God, because that alone is the hallmark of the Holy Spirit's activity. The vitality of a church then is not measured by its size, or the commitment of its members. Nor are its doctrinal soundness, its prosperity, or even its manifestation of spiritual gifts the ultimate criteria of its worth, before God. All these goals or standards are nothing, without love.

LOVE ALONE TRIUMPHS (VV. 4-7)

Although this paragraph has often been called a pen-picture of Christian love (agape), and therefore of the Lord Jesus Christ himself, it is striking that Paul makes his points partly through negatives, by telling us what love is not. This is because he is correcting the faults of the Corinthian church, in which so many of the attitudes and actions which love contradicts seem perversely to have been thriving. It is precisely because they were envious and proud, impatient and self-seeking that Paul wrote as he did. Christian love is the Holy Spirit's great contradiction of the "natural man", of our unredeemed, fallen human nature. We must not imagine that when the Corinthian church heard Paul's words read to them they went away saying what marvellous poetry or what sublime thoughts he had written. The Spirit's purpose in inspiring Paul to write this chapter was to cut them to the quick, to bring them to recognise how very far short of God's standards they were falling, and how ignorant and complacent they were about it. Whatever wider application we may give this paragraph, its primary reference remains to the exercise of spiritual gifts within the body of believers, the way we get on with each other in the church family. "Knowledge puffs up, but love builds up" (1 Cor. 8:1). That is why the gifts are given – to build up the church – so they must be exercised in love. It is the Spirit's life-style.

As we unpack the meaning of Paul's description, we may well find our own relationships coming under the searchlight of God's Word. Love is patient, or long suffering. It does not lose its cool, whatever it may have to put up with from others, as we try to move forward in our service for the Lord. It is kind, which is the positive counterpart. Love does good even to those who do harm. Immediately, we realise that it is centred on others, rather than on the self. The opposite of love is not so much hate as self-love. That is what kills so many personal relationships – marriages, friendships, churches. When I start to move away from asking "What can I give?" or "How can I help?" to "What am I getting" and "Am I being appreciated?", I am moving away from love, and becoming pre-occupied with me.

Love does not envy. It doesn't always think itself inferior and wish that it was somebody else. Rather, it accepts and uses the gifts God has given, thankful to have them and not grudgingly wishing that they were different. At the other end of the spectrum, love does not boast, or brag. It is not proud, or puffed up. Christians who use their gifts, in love, do not draw attention to themselves and how "gifted" they are. They are not windbags, advertising their self-importance. They are not name droppers, always rehearsing their successes and the influence they are having. They do not blow their own trumpets. Loving servers want to be hidden behind Christ's cross. They want people to whom they minister to see Jesus, not them. It is impossible to serve others in love and to be proud. The Spirit is self-effacing.

Love is not rude. The word means riding roughshod over someone, treating them unfairly, taking advantage of them. This is the sort of "gift" or "ministry" which drives its hearers into the ground, which is totally lacking in sensitivity towards others and which will neither listen nor learn. Such "service" shows that self, not Christ, is in the driving seat. But real love is not self seeking. Churches are so often split over the use of spiritual gifts, because they become a battle ground for a power contest. Somebody wants to have his own little empire, to be the big fish, however small the pool. But all such control-freakery is the very opposite of the Christ who chose to do the Father's will and even to give himself up for us all.

Often a gifted Christian challenges others for the leadership of the group. He or she constantly wants the pre-eminence, to be up-front, to be heard, to have their say and ultimately their own way. It is all dressed up in spiritual clothes, of course, but at root it is self-seeking. "We need freedom to exercise our gifts, to develop a deeper spirituality, to move on in the Spirit." Any of these sentiments might be valid, but Paul's point is that you know by the way it is done whether it is of God, or not. Love is the Spirit's life-style; a love that is patient and kind, and that does not ride roughshod over others. Without it, what may sound so spiritual and plausible is actually saying, " I want to be the king pin. If you don't play the game the way I want, I'm taking my bat home and my friends with me and we won't play at all!" Such behaviour may boost an ego, but it doesn't build the church. Actually, it reflects the immaturity of the primary school playground.

Love is not easily angered, not easily provoked. It is not touchy. Love has a long fuse. Some Christians ought to wear a label saying, "Danger! High Explosive." They are always blowing up if they are not appreciated as they think they should be or if their desires are being frustrated. That is never the fruit of the Spirit of love. Love keeps no record of wrongs. It wipes the slate clean, just as Jesus has done for us. It does not go in for action replays of other people's past mistakes, or failures. It does not treasure up grievances or hold grudges. It never says, "I'll forgive but I won't forget." Love is the Spirit's life-style.

Love does not delight in evil but rejoices with the truth. At first sight, this may seem a strange statement for Paul to make. Why ever would a Christian "delight in evil"? Perhaps the point is that he does not recognise the evil for what it is. It would be easy to dismiss the previous two verses with their catalogue of loveless behaviour as just minor weaknesses, or personality faults that we all have. To see them as evil is a different matter. But that's the conclusion I must come to when I rejoice in the truth of God's Word, however personally painful such a discovery may be to me. If I am not personally humbled under God's Word, I shall never realise how totally dependent I am upon God's love. Only then shall I be able to have a right attitude towards my fellow Christians. If we are called upon to admonish or rebuke one another, we must remember how much we need love to do it in Christ's way. Otherwise we soon become superior or censorious. It is not love's character to be always tracking down and pointing out what is wrong in others. Its impetus is always to rejoice in what is right and so to be a means of strength and encouragement.

As we have already noted frequently, the Bible will allow no divisions between truth and love. One of the practical reasons, evident here in the Corinthian church, is that love must be genuine, something which can only be proved by its truth content. This is even more the case in our own contemporary culture, when "love" has become the most flexible of words, with an impossibly wide spectrum of meanings. In English we are at a considerable disadvantage since we have only the one word to represent that whole range, whereas in Greek there is a wider terminology, which explains why Christian love is always referred to as "agape". It is a distinct term for a distinct love, which derives its very essence from the God who is ultimate and absolute Truth.

This is a significant consideration because a simple statement such as "God is love" will often be given an almost limitless flexibility of definition, unless its terms are firmly controlled by the content of Biblical revelation. Not only does this result in the words of Scripture being devalued, until they are virtually meaningless, but it also opens the way for all sorts of other Biblical truths to be contradicted by this revised and limited interpretation. One of the ways of ensuring that we are on track in understanding the Bible is to recognise that Scripture always agrees with Scripture and interprets the whole consistently.

For example, it would be a misuse of the central concept of love, revealed in the character of God, to suppose that this denies the ingredient of penal substitution in the atoning sacrifice of Christ on the cross. To think that a wrathful Father could punish his Son, as an innocent third party, for the sins of the human race, it is argued, is a denial both of God's justice and his love. The phrase "cosmic child abuse" has been used of this orthodox, Biblical teaching about the cross. But that emotive terminology cannot obscure the testimony of Scripture that "God was in Christ reconciling the world to himself" (2 Cor. 5:19), that the Father and the Son were united in their commitment to the atoning substitutionary death of the lamb at Calvary, or that the Son freely gave himself up for us all. We must not allow our distorted, inadequate view of God's love, due to our humanity and our sinfulness, to deny what is clearly taught as God's truth throughout the Bible.

Or again, some contemporary theologians are suggesting that the love of God is incompatible with a strong doctrine of God's sovereign role over his creation, expressed in his providence. So Scripture is pitted against Scripture. In brief, the argument is that a God who loves human beings so much as to make them in his image, with capacities which reflect his deity, including freedom of choice and action, would be merely playing games with his creation if ultimately everything was foreknown and predestined by him. Such a deity would be like a cynical puppeteer, pulling all the strings while pretending to give his creatures self-determination, and how can that possibly square with the revelation that God is love? This line of argument has led to the views of open theism, that God does not direct all things according to the counsel of his will, that he does not know the end from the beginning, that he is not in sovereign control over the whole of the created order, including the dimensions of time, along with everything to which he has given life. But that is to take one Biblical truth, the one which is not favourable to our human thinking and to use it to deny another, which is actually taught throughout Scripture (see, for example, especially the many references in Isaiah 42-48).

It is significant, of course, that it is always the freest and most self-indulgent interpretation of the love of God which wins out in such attacks on revealed truth. Whatever endorses our independence from, and rebellion against, the rule of God's truth will always be the most attractive option for our sinful human nature. But that is why we are studying the Holy Spirit's person and work as the Spirit of truth.

If love "rejoices with the truth" (v. 6) then clearly we are not free to define that love, which is the Spirit's chief fruit, in any other terms than those of the truth which he has revealed. The church at Corinth seems to have harboured completely wrong ideas about the nature of "agape". They were not ignorant of the concept, of course. They knew the terminology only too well, but they were giving it entirely the wrong, self-indulgent content. Their wrong ideas about love flowed out into the wrong practices in the life-style of the congregation and especially in the misuse of the "charismata", which focus the major corrective purpose Paul has in writing this section of the letter. We must not fall into the tempting contemporary versions of the same fatal error.

Love always protects, trusts, hopes and perseveres. This is the Spirit's life-style. Christian love upholds and supports everyone within the fellowship, in every situation. It never loses faith. This does not mean that Christian love is endlessly gullible, but, in Calvin's words, "it would rather be deceived by its gentleness of heart than injure a brother by suspicion." The characteristic of love is that it is always ready to think the best, to put the most favourable construction on everything. This is why love never fails. It is indestructible; nothing can overcome it. No hardship or rebuff ever makes such love stop loving. The essence of "agape", the distinctive New Testament term which originates in and is modelled on God's love for us, is that it looks neither for worthiness in the object of its love nor for reciprocation from it. God loves because he is love (1 John 4:8,16) and we love because he first loved us. That is why whatever gifts we may have and whatever service we may render, it will be of no value at all, unless it is energised by God's own love. We are to serve the Lord in his way, through his power, and that will always mean in love.

LOVE ALONE ENDURES (vv. 8-13)

The final way in which Paul highlights the superiority of love is to show that even the greatest gifts are temporal. They are tied to this passing world, and so they are bound to be imperfect. They will, therefore, cease; but love will never fail. Verses 9-12 expound the theme. Someday our present partial knowledge and prophesying will be replaced by the perfect, the complete. This is illustrated by the picture of a child who as a mark of maturity gives up infant thought and speech for the thought and speech of an adult (v. 11). All our gifts in this world will be seen to be childish babble in comparison with the completeness of the world to come. Our present perceptions and knowledge are imperfect because they are indirect ("but a poor reflection" v. 12a), but one day when we see the Lord "face to face" we shall know him fully, as he knows us through and through even now. The gifts are needed now, and graciously provided by God, to meet certain needs, but at their very best they can do so only imperfectly. When perfection comes, they will be obsolete. But love will not! That is Paul's point in verse 13. Love alone remains eternally.

Both the Corinthian Christians and we, in the contemporary church, need to put our interest in spiritual gifts, and our use of them, into this perspective. It will save us from becoming preoccupied with the transient. The mirror image (v. 12) is indirect and it is incomplete. You can only see what lies within the borders of the mirror. The prophet learns, or sees, only a glimpse of part of the reality; it is very limited (v. 9). No one can see all of God's plan, or understand all of God's will. Even prophecy, the one gift which Paul especially exhorts the Corinthians to desire eagerly in 14:1, is only a partial, temporary substitute for the full and complete knowledge which will one day be ours (v. 10a).

As so often in his writings, the apostle is driving us towards the great day of Christ's coming, the future horizon which will see the consummation of all things. A great deal of the difficulty at Corinth (as today) was rooted in an inability or unwillingness to distinguish between the "now" and the "not yet". In their boasting about their gifts, the church at Corinth seems to have fooled itself into believing that all the blessings of the future kingdom had come into their present experience. How wrong can you be? Surely, this was an example of their pride which prevented them from seeing clearly. Paul's argument is that gifts will cease. They are part of this world, not of the eternal realities. How foolish it would be, then, to major on what is temporal and transient, rather than on the eternal reality of love. That will never end. Even now faith, hope and love matter more than gifts or ministries. But faith will be replaced by sight and hope will be lost in fulfilment. Only love lasts for ever, because it is the currency of heaven, the Spirit's life-style. The Kingdom of God is eternal, present-tense love, which is why love is the most excellent way.

> "Love ever lives, forgives, outlives,
>
> And ever stands, with open hands,
>
> And while it lives, it gives,
>
> And while it gives, it lives,
>
> For this is love's prerogative -
>
> To give and give and give."

8.

EVANGELISM
- THE SPIRIT'S HEART-BEAT

ACTS 2:1-41

When the day of Pentecost came, they were all together in one place. Suddenly a sound like the blowing of a violent wind came from heaven and filled the whole house where they were sitting. They saw what seemed to be tongues of fire that separated and came to rest on each of them. All of them were filled with the Holy Spirit and began to speak in other tongues as the Spirit enabled them. Now there were staying in Jerusalem God-fearing Jews from every nation under heaven. When they heard this sound, a crowd came together in bewilderment, because each one heard them speaking his own language. Utterly amazed, they asked: "Are not all these men who are speaking Galileans? Then how is it that each of us hears them in his own native language? Parthians, Medes and Elamites; residents of Mesopotamia, Judea and Cappodocia, Pontus and Asia, Phrygia and Pamphylia, Egypt and the part of Libya near Cyrene;

visitors from Rome (both Jews and converts to Judaism); Cretans and Arabs – we hear them declaring the wonders of God in our own tongues!" Amazed and perplexed, they asked one another, "What does this mean?" Some, however, made fun of them and said, "They have had too much wine." (Acts 2:1-13)

No book on the Holy Spirit could possibly be complete without a section dealing with the magnificent second chapter of Acts. The great events in Jerusalem on the Day of Pentecost have often been referred to as the birthday of the church. The scene was dramatic and unforgettable. The group of believers, numbering about a hundred and twenty (Acts 1:15), who were filled with the Holy Spirit that day, were totally transformed by God's life-changing dynamic. Just a few weeks earlier, the inner core of disciples had been huddled together, doors shut for fear of the Jews, desperately afraid that they might follow their Lord and master to execution. But the risen Lord came to them, to show them his wounded body as incontrovertible proof that he was indeed alive, the conqueror of death. For forty days he lived among them, instructing them in his truth and assuring them of his love. Then, suddenly, he was gone. Acts 1:9-11 records the historic event of his ascension, taken from them into heaven.

The disciples were left on earth, but not just with wonderful memories. They had a commission and a promise. The commission was to be his witnesses to the ends of the earth. The promise was that they would receive power, the ability to fulfil the task, "when the Holy Spirit comes on you" (Acts 1:8). Clearly, these parting words of Jesus, recorded by Luke, were one of his major teaching themes, during his last days with them. Matthew also records the same emphasis as the climax to his Gospel (28:18-20). This time the location was a mountain in Galilee where Jesus had arranged to meet them. The commission was to go and make disciples of all nations, teaching them to obey everything Christ had commanded. The promise was that he would certainly be with them always, to the very end of the age.

But he was about to return to heaven, so how could he be with them? Doubtless their minds went to the promise of another counsellor, the gift of the Father, the promised Holy Spirit. He would be the divine enabling to get the task done, and Pentecost was the start of the fulfilment. Previously fearful and withdrawn, the disciples were overwhelmed by the energy of God, the Holy Spirit, filling them with his own life, and thrusting them out among the gathering crowds in Jerusalem that festival morning, to declare the wonders of God (v. 11). The power of the Spirit is given with a view to world-wide mission. That is the contents page of the book of Acts – "in Jerusalem, and in all Judea and Samaria, and to the ends of the earth" (1:8). It is the heart-beat of the Spirit, because above everything else, lost people matter to God.

There is a wonderful inclusiveness about Luke's account of the great visitation of the Spirit that day. All the believers were together, in one place (v. 1). They were being obedient to the Lord's command not to leave Jerusalem, but to wait for the Father's gift. The whole house where they were sitting was filled with the rushing wind from heaven (v. 2). The fiery tongues rested on each one (v. 3). All were filled with the Holy Spirit and all became Christ's witnesses as they spoke in other languages, according to the words the Spirit gave them to speak out. Within a few verses, Peter becomes their spokesman, preaching the great gospel sermon which we will examine later, but Luke is making an important theological point when he draws our attention to the fact that all were filled and that all were verbal witnesses. The presence of the Spirit in power was evidenced by a declaration of the wonders of God, in words that people could understand. "We hear them declaring the wonders of God in our own tongues!" (v. 11).

What we see happening at Pentecost is the reversal of the effect caused by the rebellion of the Tower of Babel, recorded in Genesis 11:1-9. In that brief but vivid Old Testament story we see all the pride of the human heart in its rebellion against God. The very essence of sin is laid bare. Man will build his own stairway to heaven, by his own unaided activity. Humanity will declare its independence of its creator and make its own way in God's world. But God came down in judgment to scatter the human race and confuse its languages so that they could no longer understand one another and thus form a cohesive, one-world rebellion against God. Of course, that remains the great objective of the anti-Christ, but the forces of evil always tend towards fragmentation and self-destruction by their very nature. Only love can unite, and only God is the source of love, as we saw in the last chapter. When the Spirit came to reverse the Babel-effect, by miraculous gift, the different languages of the world were united, as the Pentecost disciples proclaimed the wonders of God to the multi-cultural congregation gathered in Jerusalem. It was the clearest possible sign that God could have given, to indicate that the gospel of his Son, Jesus Christ, is for the whole world. The gift of tongues, or languages, was not given for private praise, but for public proclamation. The Spirit's heart-beat is always for a lost world.

'Then Peter stood up with the Eleven, raised his voice and addressed the crowd: "Fellow Jews and all of you who live in Jerusalem, let me explain this to you; listen carefully to what I say. These men are not drunk, as you suppose. It's only nine in the morning! No, this is what was spoken by the prophet Joel:

"In the last days, God says, I will pour out my Spirit on all people. Your sons and daughters will prophesy, your young men will see visions, your old men will dream dreams. Even on my servants, both men and women, I will pour out my Spirit in those days, and they will prophesy. I will show wonders in the heaven above and signs on the earth below, blood and fire and billows of smoke. The sun will be turned to darkness and the moon to blood before the coming of the great and glorious day of the Lord. And everyone who calls on the name of the Lord will be saved."' (Acts 2:14-21)

At this point in the narrative, Luke begins to stress that the personal witness of each believer had to be focused by an authoritative explanation of the event and its significance, from the lips of Peter, as spokesman. Both levels of evangelism have always been needed and provided for, by the power of the Spirit, throughout the history of the church. It is still so today. If you visit effective churches, in Britain or all over the world, you will invariably discover that personal witness and public proclamation go hand in hand. Where Christians trust the Spirit's power to enable them to build loving, meaningful relationships, and where they are able and willing to make a verbal witness to their faith in Christ, there you have wide open doors for the gospel. Where this is combined with proclamation that is uncompromisingly Biblical in its content and contemporary in its application, combined with authentic loving relationships among the Christians, there you find God adding to the church regularly those who are being saved.

Peter's method in these verses repays careful study. He starts where his hearers are, with all their misunderstandings and false ideas. There were some who were only too happy to poke fun at what was happening and to attribute the effects to too much wine (v. 13). So, Peter starts there and with a common-sense reference to the fact that it's only early morning, he begins to explain the event in Biblical terms by referring to the Old Testament prophet, Joel. It is actually a classic model of Bible teaching method. The Scriptures themselves are a record of what God has said and done, throughout revelatory history. We often speak of them as teaching God's truth and being the source of sound doctrine, but surprisingly little of that teaching is in straightforward theological propositions. Even the New Testament letters were frequently generated as apostolic responses to events which had happened in the churches, usually the invasion of false teachers. In large tracts of the Biblical

113

landscape, therefore, the revelation consists in the recounting of divine events together with the divine explanation of their meaning and significance. Almost instinctively, it would seem, but surely under the Spirit's controlling power, Peter uses exactly that method here.

In using the prophecy of Joel 2:28-32, Peter is explaining that the events of Pentecost have both a particular and a universal reference. We have just been told that he was filled with the Holy Spirit (v. 4), so we can be quite sure that what we have here is the authoritative, divinely-inspired interpretation of this climactic event. If that is so, then we do not need any contemporary alternatives or modified views, for what God said he still says. The Spirit's descent in power is rooted in the Old Testament where prophecy, visions and dreams were the normal modes of God's revelation, but almost always to specific individuals. They may have been the channel of that revelation to others – kings, generals, elders, even the whole nation. This manifestation of the Spirit at Pentecost, however, heralds "the last days", in which all of God's people receive the indwelling power of the Spirit and become messengers of the divine Word of truth. Revelation is no longer restricted to Israel alone. The Spirit is poured out on all flesh, all the nations (v. 17). Old and young, men and women are all included in this outpouring, with the effect that they will prophesy (v. 18). Just as God's truth is revealed for the whole world, so those who receive that truth declare to the world what God has done in Jesus Christ. That will be the content of Peter's great sermon.

Luke's message is clear. In the Word of the gospel of Christ, we have the sure and certain revelation of God. He, who spoke throughout history, has said a final word to mankind, in Christ – the Word who became flesh (John 1:14). In his grace and mercy, God has not left his world in the dark, but he has revealed himself to all people everywhere, in terms that everyone can understand – a truly human life. God's truth is not enshrined in philosophical formulations or theological propositions, but in his Son. It is truth, in love. "In the past, God spoke to our forefathers through the prophets at many times and in various ways, but in these last days he has spoken to us by his Son, whom he appointed heir of all things, and through whom he made the universe. The Son is the radiance of God's glory and the exact representation of his being, sustaining all things by his powerful word." (Heb. 1:1-3). Notice again the reference to "the last days", which is the terminology consistently used by the New Testament writers to refer to the period between the first and second comings of Christ. They are the last days because God's saving revelation is complete and all that the world now awaits is the climax of history, in the return of the King.

We must not lose sight of the personal implications of all this. If we have received the good news of Christ's salvation then we are called upon to proclaim that message, by life and words, in the power of the Spirit. Every Christian is involved, not just a special group of preachers, evangelists or church leaders. All Christians now prophesy, because we are all capable of receiving and passing on the unchanging revelation of God's truth in the gospel. That is why the enabling power of the Holy Spirit is given to us. This is the great sign of the gospel age, to be linked with the cataclysmic upheavals of the last days referred to in verses 19-20, but all these gospel signs are designed to produce the outcome of verse 21. "Everyone who calls on the name of the Lord will be saved". This is our commission for which we need both the gospel truth and the enabling power of the Spirit. We have no permission to decide to major on one or the other, to opt for Word or Spirit, doctrine or experience, mind or heart, truth or love. Only when the two strands are combined together do we have authentic New Testament Christianity.

Indeed, the whole chapter we are studying is a powerful example of this very point. Until verse 21 the concentration has been almost exclusively on the coming of the Spirit and his work in and through those whom he filled. But with the mention of salvation at the end of the quotation from Joel, the focus changes to the Word of the gospel, and for the next fifteen verses Peter's sermon outline is given to us as a magnificent example of preaching the objective gospel message, which is the characteristic of true inspiration by the Holy Spirit.

"Men of Israel, listen to this: Jesus of Nazareth was a man accredited by God to you by miracles, wonders and signs, which God did among you through him, as you yourselves know. This man was handed over to you by God's set purpose and foreknowledge; and you, with the help of wicked men, put him to death by nailing him to the cross. But God raised him from the dead, freeing him from the agony of death, because it was impossible for death to keep its hold on him. David said about him:

'I saw the Lord always before me. Because he is at my right hand, I will not be shaken. Therefore my heart is glad and my tongue rejoices; my body also will live in hope, because you will not abandon me to the grave, nor will you let your Holy One see decay. You have made known to me the paths of life; you will fill me with joy in your presence.

Brothers, I can tell you confidently that the patriarch David died and was buried, and his tomb is here to this day. But he was a prophet and knew that God had promised him on oath that he would place one of his descendants on his throne. Seeing what was ahead, he spoke of the resurrection of the Christ, that he was not abandoned to the grave, nor did his body see decay. God has raised this Jesus to life, and we are all witnesses of the fact. Exalted to the right hand of God, he has received from the Father the promised Holy Spirit and has poured out what you now see and hear. For David did not ascend to heaven, and yet he said,

The Lord said to my Lord: 'Sit at my right hand until
I make your enemies a footstool for your feet.'"

Therefore let all Israel be assured of this: God has
made this Jesus, whom you crucified, both Lord and
Christ." (Acts 2:22-36)

As with every Biblical event, there is a particularity to its
circumstances and context which means that it can never be
repeated. But the essential substance of Peter's content provides
us with a model for gospel proclamation, in every place, at any
time. We live in a totally different context. While he spoke to Jews
and God-fearers, nurtured in the Old Testament scriptures, we
speak largely to those who are grossly ignorant of the contents
of the Bible. Recent surveys indicate widespread ignorance of
the most famous stories from the life of Jesus, of the Lord's
prayer, even of the events of Christmas and Easter, especially
among the under 25's. I remember a university student who
said he could not believe in Christ "because of all that stuff
in the Old Testament". Asked if it was the creation story that
bothered him, he replied, "No, it was Noah and the flood". "Do
you find it hard to accept a universal flood?" I enquired. No"
he responded, "that's not my problem. It's that bit where, after
the flood, Noah comes out of the ark and throws stones over
his shoulders, and they turn into people." He was genuinely
amazed to be unable to find that part of the story in Genesis.
He was sure someone had told him it. And that was his number
one reason for not trusting Christ!

We may not launch into extensive quotation of Psalms 16 or
110, as Peter did. We shall probably want, and need, to start a lot
further back than that with our contemporary hearers, but this
sermon shows us what are the continuing priorities of the Holy
Spirit for evangelistic witness, and they cut across many of our
unquestioned contemporary presuppositions. What message does
the Spirit give and what content is he committed to honour?

Verses 22-24 are remarkably tightly packed, but there is no
doubt at all about their central theme – the person of the Lord
Jesus Christ. He is the gospel. Notice four things that Spirit-
filled evangelism will always stress about Jesus.

i)   *His historicity.* The fact that "Jesus of Nazareth was a man." (v. 22) still needs to be affirmed. No one who heard Peter that day doubted it, but we still run into people who have no idea how well established the historicity of Jesus is. Rousseau put it well when he said that if Jesus Christ did not exist, then the mind that made him up would have had to be just as great as his mind was, and whose mind was it? The reliability of the New Testament manuscripts, the evidence of secular historians and of archeological discoveries, the very existence of the Christian church itself all combine to underline the authenticity of the person of Jesus. There are excellent treatments of this sort of evidence readily available in Professor Sir Norman Anderson's *Christianity: the Witness of History* or Bishop Paul Barnett's book *Is the New Testament true?*

ii)   *His miraculous works.* Again, Peter had the advantage over us in that he was speaking to people who knew all about what God had done through the ministry of Jesus. His point is therefore not that the miracles happened, but that through them Jesus was "accredited by God". It is significant that during Christ's lifetime and the decades immediately following, there is no record of any of his opponents attempting to deny the factual basis of the miracle stories. They attributed his powers to the occult (Beelzebub) or to magic, learned in Egypt, but they could not deny that the miracles occurred. Too many people had seen them and knew those who had benefited from them.

Peter calls the miracles "wonders and signs", terms which have a long and important Old Testament pedigree. They are particularly applied to the greatest manifestation of the power of God in the creation of the old covenant people through the deliverance from Egypt, by his mighty hand, in the events of Exodus (eg Deut. 26:8). In the context of this Old Testament Jewish background, Peter is clearly claiming that the works of Jesus are equivalent to, or even greater than, the exodus events, in terms of their significance for the people of God. They are the indisputable evidence of the mighty hand of God. Similarly, John's Gospel is built around the concept of the seven "signs", pointing to Christ's identity and climaxing in the resurrection. All this is irrefutable evidence of Jesus' deity.

Just as Old Testament believers were called upon to exercise their faith by remembering how God had redeemed his people from Egypt (and unbelief is precisely a failure to remember), so New Testament faith is grounded in the historical acts of redemption brought about by Jesus Christ, and attested by the miraculous signs which he alone performed. To demand additional contemporary signs and wonders, as a condition of belief in Christ, may actually be to expose our fundamental unbelief. God has already accredited Jesus of Nazareth, by his mighty deeds, and there are no competitors. While we can and do rejoice in every evidence of God's mercy in healing today, we cannot pretend that anyone, anywhere, is doing or ever has done the mighty things Christ did, which were the revelation of his divine power. Whether privately to the disciples, as when he walked on the water, or publicly to the crowds, as when he fed the 5,000 with one boy's lunch, Jesus declared his uniqueness as the Son of God. If the apostolic testimony is not sufficient for our faith then we condemn ourselves to remain unbelievers. Indeed, their own testimony was also going to be accredited by God in "signs and wonders" (Acts 2:43, 5:12, 14:3, 15:12) but clearly these were tied directly to the first generation of eye-witnesses, directly commissioned by the risen Lord. They were supremely the marks of the apostles (Rom. 15:19, 2 Cor. 12:12) whose witness served as the proclamation of the great saving event that we call the gospel.

iii)   *His death and resurrection.* Not surprisingly, the signs of Christ's ministry culminate in the cross and the empty tomb. In verse 23, Peter stresses that the death of Jesus was not a ghastly mistake, or a tragic miscalculation. It was not that he over-reached himself. Nor even that he gave his life as a moral example, the supreme pattern of self-sacrifice. All of these, and many other theories of the cross, have been advanced down the years to try to explain the enigma of Calvary. Why should such a transparently good man die such a horrific and apparently meaningless death? "What a pity Jesus died as such a young man", a lady once confided in me. "If only he had lived until he was eighty, think of all the good he could have done in the world!" You have to say something like that, if you don't have the divine explanation of the event given by Peter in this text.

The message of the apostolic gospel is that the cross of Christ was no accident. It was both because of "God's set purpose and foreknowledge" and because of human sin. It was a death at the hands of sinners ("wicked men") yet on behalf of sinners. At this point in the unfolding story of the church, Peter does not preach a fully-developed doctrine of the atonement. It is enough for him to demonstrate the guilt of his hearers in their complicity with the death of Christ – "you ... put him to death". Our evangelistic explanations will need to unpack the significance of substitutionary sacrifice, so familiar to Peter's Jewish hearers that it could be taken as read, as soon as anyone began to speak of a death on behalf of others. But in our solidarity with Adam as sinful human beings it is surely not stretching Peter's meaning too far twenty centuries later to agree that there is a sense in which we too have crucified the Lord of glory. Our sinful human hearts are no different from theirs. We too in our culture are only too keen to shout "Away with him! We will not have this man to reign over us." By a thousand acts of rebellion and sinfulness we too crucify our king. There can be no twenty-first century experience of forgiveness, without a conviction and confession of sin and guilt. And that will only become real when we understand the meaning of the cross. This is Spirit-directed evangelism.

Linked indissolubly to the cross in all the apostolic preaching is the fact of the resurrection. In verse 24, Peter emphasises that this is the ultimate sign, the vindication of all that Jesus claimed and the proof of his divine identity. He stresses its theological inevitability. How could death hold captive the one who, by his dying, had conquered all the hostile forces ranged against our humanity? David's prophetic word in Psalm 16:8-11 had promised as much, and Peter quotes it extensively, under the inspiration of the Holy Spirit, to demonstrate how the greatest of Israel's kings foresaw a day when one of his descendents would be enthroned as God's everlasting king. "God has raised this Jesus [great David's greater son] to life and we are all witnesses of the fact" (v. 32). We believe because they saw. Our faith is not wishful thinking, nor is it based on rumour or hear-say evidence. It is grounded in the facts of Christ's historical death and resurrection, God's greatest intervention in history, to save a lost world. It is guaranteed by the testimony of apostolic eye-witnesses, many of whom died as martyrs rather than deny what they knew to be the truth.

iv) *His exaltation and sovereign rule.* Once again, Peter's emphasis is squarely on historical events. The Christ who rose ascended to the position of sovereign authority at "the right hand of God". The apostles had seen him go, but how could Peter know what had happened next? The answer is the events of Pentecost morning. Here was the fulfilment of the promise made by the one who claimed to have all authority in heaven, as well as on earth (Matt 28:18). The gift of the Spirit was not a private ecstasy for the chosen few, it was as much a public event as the cross or the empty tomb. These things were not done in a corner. So, Peter brings the events the crowd were witnessing ("what you now see and hear") right in to the main stream of salvation history and affirms that the gift of the Spirit is the clinching testimony to the authority of Jesus Christ, as king and conqueror, judge and returning Lord. This is the thrust of the further Davidic quote (vv. 34-35), this time from one of the great messianic psalms, 110 .

All this Spirit-inspired, gospel proclamation reaches its climax in the ringing declaration of verse 36. This crucified Jesus is both Lord and Christ. His full title encapsulated in that magnificent statement is the essential message we have to declare to the world. Jesus of Nazareth, Son of David, Son of God, anointed King, is Lord. That is the good news, with which came forgiveness, peace, reconciliation and eternal life. There could be no clearer demonstration possible that the great work of the Holy Spirit is to uplift the Lord Jesus and draw men and women to his feet in wonder, love and praise.

As we reflect on this model of evangelistic communication, we need to put our contemporary presentations of the gospel alongside Peter's message, so as to assess how faithful we are to the apostolic precedent. If this is the example of the Holy Spirit's inspiration in evangelism, given that it was "targeted" to a particular audience at a particular time, are there enduring lessons we can learn? In an age which is particularly interested in methods, often at the expense of content, the question becomes vital. The great danger in evangelicalism today is that pragmatism will take us over. Whatever seems "to work" is presumed to be acceptable because God appears to be "blessing" it. But we do need to make sure that we are not subtly diluting, or even distorting, the apostolic message. There are three challenging contrasts we need to highlight between what we know here as Spirit-directed evangelism and some of our contemporary practices.

Firstly, with regard to the message. Peter's preaching is not Jesus is great, but Jesus is Lord. Or to put it another way, his emphasis is not on testimony but on truth. Evangelism is the declaration of an unchanging message regarding the person and work of Jesus Christ. It has a "givenness", an objectivity about its content. Too often in our desperate attempt to make our message "relevant" we simply talk about our personal experience of Jesus, and we can end up almost recommending Christianity as our particular brand from the shelves of the world's ideological supermarket. But the Lord Jesus is not one religious hero among many, one product we might care to sample. He is Lord, and the gospel message is a summons to submit to his kingly authority now, before it is experienced as judgment and eternal condemnation. If "evangelism" becomes an appeal to give Jesus a try, we all know what happens, though we often don't trace later problems back sufficiently to their roots. Those who respond do so on their terms, rather than God's. They become fair weather followers who contract out when Christ's teaching and demands start to cross their presuppositions and conflict with their priorities. This sort of evangelism can never call disciples to take up the cross and follow Christ.

Then, with regard to its focus, Peter's preaching is not need-centred, but Christ-centred. This is a point that must be made insistently, as it is so easily misunderstood. Of course, all our evangelism must be related to real people where they are, with all their needs and concerns. The Bible is no supporter of expounding theological abstractions into a vacuum, nor am I arguing for that. But our natural tendency, as human beings, is to be self-centred and that is certainly intensified in an age as self-indulgent as our own. The questions our hearers will naturally begin to ask when they start to listen seriously to an evangelistic presentation are of this order. Can I accept this sort of God? What will he do for me, if I do accept him? Do I like what I'm hearing? Does it "grab" me? Am I comfortable with it? Such questions are very characteristic of our culture, not to say conditioned by it.

The problem is that they are not the questions which the Holy Spirit puts to the hearers of God's word. The gospel questions are of this order. "Is there any way in which a holy God could begin to accept me? Is this analysis of my state before him, as a guilty sinner, true? Is Jesus Christ really who he claimed to be? What must I do to be saved?" That cry was the indicator that the Holy Spirit was at work (v. 37). Peter's hearers, cut to the heart, cried out "What shall we do?" If we focus solely on the "felt needs" of our hearers, we may build bridges of relevance, but what traffic will cross them?

Hearers will tend to imagine that the gospel is a panacea for those needs. When you are feeling lonely, Jesus will be your friend. When you are feeling discouraged, Jesus will pick you up. When your life is lacking zip, Jesus will add the sparkle. Do you see how me-centred this concentration on our felt needs can become? Spirit-led evangelism must move from that initial contact to our unfelt-needs, which are actually much greater – the needs of forgiveness and peace with God. It was not Christ the panacea, the pick-me-up, or the psychological prop whom the apostles proclaimed, but Christ the Saviour, the Ruler and the Sovereign. Our greatest human need is not to feel good, but to be forgiven.

Finally, in terms of its effect, Peter's preaching centres not on our commitment, but on God's grace. The whole sermon was about God's initiative in the work of salvation from start to finish. We have to tell that story. Whether people like it or not, whether they accept it or not, the Holy Spirit is constantly witnessing to the reality of the person of Christ, as Saviour and Lord. We are not at liberty to change God's agenda. Spirit-led evangelism instructs people in the facts of what has happened, so that they can respond to the fulness of God's self-revelation, in Jesus Christ, on a basis of understanding. The Jesus of history is the Christ of faith. The Christ whom we meet in the pages of the gospels is the living Lord who transforms the life of everyone who will repent and trust in him.

Increasingly, today, we are aware that such an approach takes considerable time. As people have less and less Christian background, so-called "sudden" conversions become rarer. The journey to faith starts much further back, in this generation, than it did even twenty years ago. Terms have to be explained. The gospel story has to be taught and in it all we have to centre, as Peter did, on what God has already accomplished, in Christ. When it comes to the plan of salvation for a lost world, God is the author and prime mover (v. 22). He planned the cross (v. 23), and raised Jesus to be both Lord and Christ (v. 36).

When we preach Christ, we preach God and we preach in the strength, and with the heart-beat, of the Holy Spirit. That is why the verbs describing Peter's continuing speech ("many other words" – we only have the outline!) in verse 40 are so serious. He warned and pleaded with his hearers, and so must we. Evangelism can never be an extension of the entertainment business.

When the people heard this, they were cut to the heart and said to Peter and the other apostles, "Brothers, what shall we do?" Peter replied, "Repent, and be baptised, every one of you, in the name of Jesus Christ for the forgiveness of your sins. And you will receive the gift of the Holy Spirit. The promise is for you and your children and for all who are far off – for all whom the Lord our God will call." With many other words he warned them; and he pleaded with them, "Save yourselves from this corrupt generation." Those who accepted his message were baptised, and about three thousand were added to their number that day. (Acts 2:37-41)

Lastly, let us examine the marks of the sort of response which the Holy Spirit produces, when he is the evangelist. If the message is God-centred, then the response must be as well. There is no doubt about the serious heart-felt reaction of Peter's hearers. There was no "take it or leave it" attitude on behalf of the preacher and no such mentality in the congregation. Many knew that they had to do something about what they had heard. In the first place this meant repentance, a change of mind. It involved the recognition that they had been wrong – in their assessment of Jesus and their attitude to him, and in the way they had lived their lives without letting God have his rightful place. Repentance always involves the desire to change direction, to turn around and start going God's way. This was followed by baptism, an outward sign of the inward change. Before John the Baptist, baptism had been administered only to proselytes to Judaism, as a sign of their entry to the covenant community. John had called native Jews to be baptised in the

Jordan as a mark of their repentance, and Peter now follows the same pattern. It is the sign of the establishment of the new covenant community, and of personal membership through faith in Jesus Christ.

Repentance and faith were followed by forgiveness and the reception of the Holy Spirit (v. 38), the two always going together. The indwelling Spirit is the proof of that forgiveness, just as baptism is the outward sign of the inward work. It is very easy for us to underplay these responses, in a generation where the character of God is virtually unknown and where sin is a much diluted and rejected concept. The deep-seated hostility to God, that refuses to allow him his rights in the lives he has created, lies firmly entrenched in every human heart. That is the real issue. People may accept the historicity of Jesus, revere him as a great man, a wonderful teacher, even as a revelation of God, but they will not turn from their sin, unless the Holy Spirit enables them. The promises are secure and available for everyone who will respond to God's call (v. 39) but require acceptance of the message (v. 41) and obedience to the gospel commands.

That is why all our evangelism is so totally dependent on the Spirit's work. We proclaim and plead, we love and warn, but we are not at liberty to soft-pedal the essential message in any way. We must not be in too great a hurry to count heads. It is roots that matter, and they are the Spirit's sovereign work. He alone is the Lord and giver of life, and only he gives the increase. Our part is to proclaim the authentic message, calling on the Spirit for his power to be at work in preacher and hearers, so that there is an authentic response of repentance and faith. When it becomes the passion of our lives that lost people matter to God, we can be sure that our hearts are beating as one with the Spirit of truth.

9.
THE SPIRIT OF HOLINESS

JOHN 14:15-27

If you love me, you will obey what I command. And I will ask the Father, and he will give you another Counsellor to be with you for ever – the Spirit of truth. The world cannot accept him, because it neither sees him nor knows him. But you know him, for he lives with you and will be in you. I will not leave you as orphans; I will come to you. Before long, the world will not see me any more, but you will see me. Because I live, you also will live. On that day you will realise that I am in my Father, and you are in me, and I am in you. Whoever has my commands and obeys them, he is the one who loves me. He who loves me will be loved by my Father and I too will love him and show myself to him." Then Judas (not Judas Iscariot) said, "But, Lord, why do you intend to show yourself to us and not to the world?" Jesus replied, "If anyone loves me, he will obey my teaching. My Father will love him, and we will come to him and make our home with him. He who does not love me will not obey my teaching. These words you hear are not my own; they belong to the Father who sent me. All this I have spoken while still with you. But the Counsellor, the Holy Spirit, whom the Father will send in my name, will teach you all things and will remind you of everything I have said to you. Peace I leave with you; my peace I give you. I do not give to you as the world gives. Do not let your hearts be troubled and do not be afraid. (John 14:15-27)

When we consider the wealth of teaching given by Jesus in the Gospels, and our professed readiness to confess him as master and Lord, it is perhaps surprising how little many of us Christians actually study his words. In all the hectic activity and restlessness of modern life we need to take time to sit at his feet and listen to his teaching, and nowhere is this more the case than in what he has to say about the Holy Spirit. With all the conflicting opinions and ideas on this theme, let's ask ourselves "What does Jesus say?" And where better to turn to than John 14?

That this is a unit of teaching is made clear by the repetition of the same words at its beginning (v. 1) and end (v. 27) – "Do not let your hearts be troubled". They encapsulate all that comes in between. They also give us the context. The disciples were anxious and fearful because Jesus had told them that he was going away. Their problem was that they did not know either where he was going or how they would be able to reach him (v. 5). Not surprisingly, they found this information profoundly disturbing.

Let's put ourselves in their shoes. It has been their great privilege to live and work with the Lord Jesus for the past three years or so. During this time, they have enjoyed the amazing adventure of beginning to get to know God personally, although his glory has been veiled. Nevertheless Jesus, the Son, has introduced them to his heavenly Father and theirs. Now, suddenly, there is a threat that all of this is going to stop. Jesus is going to be removed, so how will they be able to continue their relationship with the Father? As Philip expresses their thoughts in verse 8, to see the Father would be all that anyone could possibly ask. The next verse records Jesus' gentle rebuke, which is at the same time the most tremendous claim to deity, "Anyone who has seen me has seen the Father."

But how are they to go on "seeing" the Father, if Jesus is no longer to be with them? Let's bring it right up to date. How are we to? How can any of us come to know God in a personal way, if we cannot see, talk to and listen to the Son, who came to reveal him? It is in answer to these questions that Jesus gives us this magnificent, heart-warming teaching about the Holy Spirit, who would come to them all at Pentecost. That great event would be unrepeatable, and yet Christians in every generation live in the benefit of it, for we too share in the life of the Spirit. The content here centres around two focal points – verses 16 - 18 where Jesus describes the Spirit of truth and verses 26-27 where he speaks about the Spirit of holiness.

THE SPIRIT OF TRUTH (VV. 16-18)

Verse 16 is both very rich and very fully packed. We need to remember the question Jesus is answering. When Jesus is no longer in this world, after his death on the cross, his resurrection and ascension, how will men and women be able to come to a personal knowledge of God? He has asserted in verse 6 that he alone is the way so when the way is no longer there, which will be the road to travel? The answer is that for all generations the knowledge of God will still come only through a knowledge of Jesus himself, but that this knowledge, which is "truth", ultimate and absolute, will be provided by the Spirit, whom Jesus describes as "another Counsellor".

The Greek word used here for "another" has a definition lacking in our English. It means "another of exactly the same sort". Suppose you were to break a cup which formed a part of a matching tea-set. A friend might offer to replace it. If they bought a cup that did not match the set, it would probably not be acceptable. They might argue that it was another cup, that it held tea and did the job for which it was produced equally effectively, but it would not fit or match in the same way. It would be another cup – but different. What you would want would be another of exactly the same sort, design, shape and pattern. Then, it would be indistinguishable from the original cup. That is the word Jesus uses to describe the Holy Spirit. He is "another", but of exactly the same sort as the Lord Jesus himself, equally and completely divine. The Counsellor will therefore be exactly like the one they have with them at present. What Jesus means by that is explained partly by the choice of the word and partly by the preceding verses. In verse 10, Jesus defines himself as the Father's counsellor. If, then, he is about to leave them, his disciples will need another counsellor – equally divine and equally powerful.

The Spirit pleads the Father's cause (v. 16)

The word for 'counsellor' can be transliterated into English as 'Paraclete'. Literally meaning 'called to your side to help', it corresponds exactly to the Latin *advocatus*. An advocate is someone who acts on your behalf, in a court of law. The Paraclete comes with you to court, as a friend to testify to your character, to your value as an honest and reliable citizen, to persuade the justices on your behalf. So if justice is to be done, it is essential that the advocate should speak the truth. He is the witness to reality. In the same way, the Holy Spirit is portrayed here as the Father's witness or advocate. Just as Jesus, the Son, came to the earth to do that (v. 11), so when he has gone, the Holy Spirit will fulfil that same role, in God's people. We are accustomed to think of the Paraclete as coming alongside us to plead our cause either to God, or perhaps to the world (in witness), but that is not what Jesus is saying here. Rather, he promises that the Spirit will plead the Father's cause, through the Son, and that explains one of the reasons why we need Him so much.

In John's Gospel, "truth" means ultimate truth, that is the essential nature of God, the divine reality. Jesus is the truth, in that absolute sense, the one who reveals God to men. To describe the Holy Spirit as the "Spirit of Truth" means that he is the Spirit of God the Father, and of Jesus Christ the Son, who reveals the nature of God to mankind and gives true witness to its ultimate and eternal reality. It is only the Holy Spirit who can open our minds, which have been blinded by sin, so that we understand who Jesus is and what he has done for us. It is only he who brings us to salvation, through Christ's death and resurrection. And it is the Spirit who creates in us a faith in Christ that is personal and life-changing. We need the Holy Spirit because only he can bring us to the knowledge of God.

He indwells the Father's children (v. 17)
In this verse Jesus draws the distinction between his disciples and the world, which is very familiar in John's Gospel. The Spirit is being given as God's free gift of himself to men and women in this world, at the request of the Lord Jesus (v. 16) and on the grounds of all that he has accomplished. But the world is unable of itself to perceive or acknowledge the Spirit's work. So, how are human lives to be open to receive the Spirit and benefit from his gracious ministry? In verse 15, Jesus has pointed to the answer. Those who truly love Christ, not just as a passing emotion or a profession of words, will prove their love by practical obedience to his commands. As we repent and believe the gospel, we begin to act on the evidence of the truth. We could never even start to do that without the Holy Spirit's gracious work within us. "No one can say, 'Jesus is Lord', except by the Holy Spirit" (1 Cor. 12:3). So even the first faintest glimmers of faith and obedience are the work of the Spirit alone. As we respond to his light, so we receive more light. As we begin to trust and obey, so the door is open for us to receive the gift of the Holy Spirit. This gift of God himself is permanent ("with you for ever", v16) and, even more wonderful, he is not just with us, but in us (v. 17b).

The departure of Jesus will not therefore leave his people bereft, like orphans (v. 18). When the Spirit comes, Jesus comes, because the Spirit is the other Jesus, of exactly the same essence and being, and he comes to bring the very life of God within the souls of men and women like us, by bringing us the truth. Indeed verse 23 speaks about the Father and the Son coming to each obedient Christian to make their home within our lives and take up permanent residence within each individual believer. When we receive the Holy Spirit at the moment of our new birth, we receive God himself – not in instalments or fragments, not to come and go, but to stay with us and to remain in us. This is what confirms that we really are Christ's disciples. The Spirit within shows us our sin, leads us to repent, assures us of our salvation, speaks his peace, guides our lives, teaches us more and more of the truth and empowers us to love and obey the Lord.

That is how, as Christians, we can enjoy more and more of the Spirit's indwelling power. Jesus stresses love (v. 15) which must issue in obedience (vv. 21, 23, 24). Keeping his commandments is the only guarantee that our love is genuine. The more we love, the more we obey, and the more we obey, the more we want to obey. We have to recognise, of course, that it is not our obedience that earns us the Spirit. We must never forget that the indwelling Spirit is the free gift of God's grace. Obedience, however, does keep the channels open, so that the Spirit can continue to work in and through our lives. If we do not obey God's Word, we shall only grieve and ultimately quench the Spirit. Because he is the "Spirit of truth", every act of disobedience is effectively a denial of the truth of God's Word, to which he testifies.

THE SPIRIT OF HOLINESS (VV. 26-27)

Verse 26 is remarkable for the way in which it so naturally embraces and unites the three persons of the Holy Trinity as one God. The reason why the Spirit of God is so often called the Holy Spirit in the Scriptures is because holiness is the supreme characteristic of God. Strictly speaking, "holiness" is not so much an attribute of God, as a word that is used to describe his essential being. It signifies his complete "otherness" from all that he has made, including humankind. It is this "set apartness" which God requires to see in his people because it reflects his own nature, the very "Godness" of God. In moral terms, the holiness of God means that he is completely sinless, since all God's moral attributes are possessed by him to an infinite degree. He is utterly righteous and pure, beyond our imagining. "He lives in unapproachable light, whom no-one has seen or can see." (1 Tim. 6:16).

When we describe the Spirit as "holy", we are affirming not only his full deity, but also that he is the one who provides holiness, who works in the lives of all who receive him, to make them like the God to whom they belong. He is sent in Christ's name to continue Christ's work in an in-depth application to our lives. If we are to become increasingly like Jesus (and that is the only objective Biblical proof that our profession of Christianity is real) we need the Holy Spirit to change us. It will be a life-long process, but how does it happen?

He instructs the disciples' minds (v. 26)
Again the words are very specific. The Spirit will be the teacher of the church, recalling Christ's teaching to her memory, explaining and interpreting his words and so enabling the church to believe and obey her master's voice. Of course, these words, as originally spoken, have a primary reference only to the apostles, whom Jesus was directly addressing, immediately before his betrayal and arrest. They were the channels of divine revelation, directly inspired by the Holy Spirit in the writing of the New Testament scriptures, as the inerrant and infallible word of God. As they wrote the four Gospels of the Lord Jesus, explained and applied in the Acts and the Epistles, they served a unique and unrepeatable function for the formation of the church. The accuracy of their remembering and the subsequent

authenticity of their written testimony is guaranteed by the coming of the Spirit as God's gift to them, and through them to every succeeding generation. We cannot remember, as they did, for we have never been the eye-witnesses and ear-witnesses which they were (2 Peter 1:16-18). Yet our remembering, while totally dependent on their authoritative witness, is just as real and vitally necessary today, in our context of discipleship, so many generations later.

The "remembering" described in this verse is not simply a feat of memory, recalling to mind something which otherwise might be forgotten. Biblical remembering is always rehearsing what has been said or done in the past with a view to present action. This is a common experience in our lives. When we remember the date of a birthday or anniversary of someone in the family, it is with a view to doing something about it. There is a card to be sent, a present to be bought, or a celebration to be arranged. When love remembers, it swings into action. Just imagine telling your wife that you remembered your wedding anniversary last week but did nothing more than make a mental note of it!

The Holy Spirit brings God's truth to our minds, explains or teaches us its meaning, with a view to encouraging us to act upon it, in detailed disciplined obedience. It is this obedience to the truth which produces holiness, or Christ-likeness of character. If the truth is not being taught, then it is impossible for holiness to develop, for Biblical holiness is not produced neither by mystical experiences, nor by internal, emotional intensity. God's truth has to grip the mind, if it is to activate the will, in order to change the life.

We can see how this works out in a very practical way by studying these three stages, as Paul outlines them, in his letter to the Ephesians. First, the truth of God has to address our minds and this is the work of the Holy Spirit. This was why he inspired the apostles to preach, teach and write the New Testament, in the first place. In the practical teaching passage beginning at

Ephesians 4:17, Paul's concern is to see a consistent and far-reaching change in the moral behaviour of Ephesian Christians ("You must no longer live as the Gentiles do, in the futility of their thinking"). The significant point is that change in behaviour begins with change in the mind. So, Paul reminds the church that their Christian discipleship began that way ("you were taught in accordance with the truth that is in Jesus" v21). It is the only way to continue. Only a mind that is responsive to the teaching of the truth, by the Holy Spirit, can produce the fruit of a holy, Christ-like life. "You were taught, with regard to your former way of life, to put off your old self, which is being corrupted by its deceitful desires; to be made new in the attitude of your minds; to put on the new self, created to be like God in true righteousness and holiness" (vv. 22-24).

How can we expect to produce a generation of Christians committed to holiness, if we do not teach God's truth in our churches, at every level? We are told today that many Christians are Biblically illiterate and that in terms of life-style it is increasingly difficult to distinguish us Christians from our unbelieving neighbours. These criticisms may well be justified, but if they are, we do not seem to have realised yet that they are directly traceable to the decline of the importance of Biblical teaching in our church life. When only a few minutes a week are considered necessary for Christian instruction, often at a superficial level and in a predominant context of entertainment, how can we expect to produce mature, godly people, who will have a lasting impact for God on our society? It is only when we are convinced in our minds of the truth, that we really become concerned about seeing it worked out in our lives. In Ephesians 4, Paul goes on to deal with the behavioural issues of lying, anger, theft, unwholesome speech, sexual impurity and greed, all on the basis of truth – who Christ is and what he has done for his people.

It is important to realise that the Biblical motivation for such a change in life-style and behaviour, which is the essence of holiness, is not law but grace; not rules but relationship. Yet so often we fail to understand this dimension of Christian living and inevitably start to drift back towards our own religious effort and works. This is particularly the case where specific instructions are rightly given, as here in Ephesians, but which can easily degenerate in our thinking to external conformity to an outward behavioural code, without any consistent recognition of the changed heart needed. Holiness is likeness of character to the Lord Jesus and that will always be the product of God's grace, through the activity of the Holy Spirit. Our problem is that we drift into legalism, because it seems to provide an acceptable level of outward conformity to the behavioural norms of the Christian sub-group to which we belong, without demanding too radical a change of our heart and affections. As soon as we become more concerned about other people's assessment of us, rather than an impassioned desire to be pleasing and acceptable to the Lord, growing into his likeness, we start to become the prisoners of a system of human achievement rather than being entirely and desperately dependent upon God's grace.

How does the Holy Spirit change this ingrained bias of our fallen human nature, with its perverse desire to be able to justify ourselves, by our knowledge, or orthodoxy, or accomplishments? Not by rules, but through deepening our relationship with him. What we find it hard to grasp is how this can happen through our study of Scripture; but that is exactly what Jesus is teaching his disciples here. As we read God's word, dependent on the illumination of the Spirit who is its primary author, he begins to stir our wills to have new concerns and desires, which reflect his nature, rather than our own sinfulness. The mind and heart of God are revealed to us, as we see his amazing grace and goodness to us in all the benefits which are ours because of the saving work of our Lord Jesus Christ.

We begin to marvel that God should love us so much as to go to such lengths of personal pain and suffering, to rescue us from sin, death and hell. We see that this great work was made necessary because of the sinless perfection and undiluted holiness of his character and we begin to realise that we are saved not only from the consequences of our sin, but to live a new life, "created to be like God in true righteousness and holiness" (Eph. 4:24). We hear the Lord Jesus teaching his disciples that love for him is evidenced in obedience to his commands (John 15:10), but it is love which is the motivation, not duty. It is our relationship with him which transforms our lives; our desire to be like the Lord who loves us so much, which leads us to those changes in behaviour and character which constitute godliness. "As obedient children, do not conform to the evil desires you had when you lived in ignorance. But just as he who called you is holy, so be holy in all you do" (1 Peter 1:14-15).

Not surprisingly then Paul also uses the truth motivationally, to stir the wills of his readers. "Be imitators of God, therefore, as dearly loved children and live a life of love, just as Christ loved us and gave himself up for us as a fragrant offering and sacrifice to God" (Eph. 5:1-2). The third and final stage follows, as Paul spells out the behavioural changes which need to take place in the lives of the Ephesian Christians. They have to establish new patterns of behaviour, which will lead to long-term character changes. What we do is the product of how we think. We do have a degree of choice in the matter, as Christians set free in Christ. The Holy Spirit can and does give us the strength to live differently, if we are prepared to obey Scripture. But there can be no compromise on that. We shall return to Paul's teaching in Ephesians 5 in our next chapter, as we consider his wisdom for life.

The Spirit governs the disciples' hearts (v. 27)
Jesus was able to bring peace to the troubled hearts of those first disciples by means of the teaching of these verses. His words of truth are his legacy of peace. How can our hearts be stable and settled in our time and place? By those same words of truth guarding our hearts and minds as we believe and obey

the teaching which the Spirit gives us through Scripture. It is characteristic of the world to give at no cost to itself. By contrast, the Lord Jesus was about to offer his life on the cross, for our peace. The world's peace ebbs and flows, but the Holy Spirit is with God's people for ever and nothing can destroy the peace he gives to those who love and obey the Lord. Every human being is looking for peace, but it is not to be found in meditative techniques or mysticism, any more than it can be found in materialism. The source of lasting peace is God alone. He is the author of all true peace and his Spirit is the channel. But just as there can be no peace without pardon, so there can be no continuing peace except on a basis of holiness. It is only by responding to the sanctifying work of the Spirit that we shall know the peace of God which defies both our analysis and our understanding.

Why do we need the Spirit? To teach us the truth in order to make us holy. He is given to every one of God's children to do just that. He is for us, with us and in us. We do not need to fear his work, or to hesitate in yielding the control-centre of our lives to him, but to let the Holy Spirit fill every area of our lives. Then we shall begin to discover the fulfilment of that deep, personal relationship with God, for which we were created, and without which we shall never be at peace.

10.
THE SPIRIT OF WISDOM

EPHESIANS 5:11-20

Have nothing to do with the fruitless deeds of
darkness, but rather expose them. For it is shameful
even to mention what the disobedient do in secret.
But everything exposed by the light becomes visible,
for it is light that makes everything visible. That is
why it is said: "Wake up, O sleeper, rise from the
dead, and Christ will shine on you." Be very careful,
then, how you live – not as unwise but as wise, making
the most of every opportunity, because the days are
evil. Therefore do not be foolish, but understand
what the Lord's will is. Do not get drunk on wine,
which leads to debauchery. Instead, be filled with the
Spirit. Speak to one another with psalms, hymns and
spiritual songs. Sing and make music in your heart
to the Lord, always giving thanks to God the Father
for everything, in the name of our Lord Jesus Christ.
(Eph. 5:11-20).

In the last chapter we looked at the work of the Spirit within
the Christian, enabling us to put off the old self and to be

made new in our minds, so that we may put on the new self. The characteristics of this new life, created to be like God, are righteousness and holiness, as Paul taught in Ephesians 4:24. But it's only too easy to agree with these great Biblical words and to adopt them into our vocabulary, without asking what they will mean in practical terms. How should we expect the life of the Spirit to be manifested in such areas as our personal relationships? What will be the practical evidences of the Spirit's work in us in terms of our everyday living? To answer these vital questions we turn back to Ephesians 5, where Paul develops his teaching on these all important issues.

LIVING AS LIGHT (vv. 11-14)

The dominant note of this paragraph is its clear-cut opposition to any form of compromise. Our life-style as Christians is to be distinctively different. We are to have no fellowship with "the fruitless deeds of darkness". The root idea of the word 'fellowship' is that we are share holders in the same concern, pooling our resources for a common aim. Clearly that cannot happen with the world, if we are true followers of Christ. There is no place at all in a disciple's life for anything that compromises the goodness, truth and righteousness which are the hallmark of our master. But although we accept that intellectually, we often argue with it in practice. That is why it is important to note the descriptive word used in verse 11 'fruitless'. Paul is not setting good fruit over against bad, but against no fruit at all. To compromise with sin is a path of total futility.

It may be helpful at this point to use our renewed minds to do some hard thinking about the process by which we, as believers, become entangled in sin. Why do we ever yield to temptation? It is only because we think that we shall be happier, more fulfilled and enriched if we follow our own desires rather than obeying God's Word. What we need to ask ourselves is whether it ever really works that way. We all know that sin never keeps its promise; its only wage is death. The devil never produces what he offers, because he is the father of lies. So we need to ask ourselves some penetrating questions.

Why do we covet, when we know that however much we may have materially, our sinful nature will always tell us it is not enough? That frustration will always exist, because material things can never satisfy our deepest human longings. Only God can do that.

Why do we worry, when we know that the only productive result is likely to be ulcers? To use up our mental and emotional energy in this destructive way never even begins to solve our problems. It simply traps us in a downward spiral of despair.

Why do we bear grudges which will only eat away at our own peace of mind and joy in life? The harboured bitterness that refuses to forget, as well as to forgive, is a killer to those who give it house room. We need to do some spiritual thinking about these issues, and so to involve our renewed minds in the battle with temptation. The light of Christ, shining from his Word, enables us to see and expose the futility of sin, which is a major step forward in winning the victory against it (v. 11b).

Of course, this is not an invitation to become moral detectives, or spiritual spies, on the sins of others; but to live such a decisively different life-style as a Christian that darkness is shown up to be what it really is – futile and fruitless. The sun rising every morning is a silent process, but it transforms everything. No one needs to blow a trumpet to tell us all that the sun has risen, because by its light everything is made visible. That is the impact our Christian lives should have on the world.

Verse 12 indicates that Paul is not thinking about the detailed denunciation of people's sins when he talks about exposing evil. Sometimes that may be needed, but words are always weak weapons in comparison with a life of unmistakable Christ-likeness. Such a life exposes evil by showing up, or making visible, what life in the darkness is really like (v. 13). Our privilege as Christians is to live in daily contact with Christ who is the light. That light must shine into our own lives firstly to expose the darkness that still lurks there and then to expel. Only then can we be reflectors of that same light of the Lord into the darkness of the world around us.

The church is to be God's light-bearer to the world. Like the moon, she shines only with a reflected light. At her most complete, the reflection is only a pale one in comparison with the light of the Son, who is our source of our energy. But a full moon transforms the darkness of night. The same idea is central to John's vision of the risen Lord in Revelation 1:12-20. The king of glory is seen among the seven golden lampstands, which symbolise the seven churches. Christ is the light, whose face is like the sun shining in all its brilliance (Rev. 1:16). But his people also carry a reflected light – they are the lampstands. So, the place where the living Lord is discovered today is among the lampstands, among his people in the churches.

When Paul told the Corinthians, "We have this treasure in jars of clay to show that this all-surpassing power is from God and not from us" (2 Cor. 4:7), he was probably thinking of the cheap earthenware lamps that could be bought in Corinth. They were fragile and easily broken, expendable even, but they carried a light. They were an equivalent to the paper cups of our twenty-first century culture – cheap and easily disposable. But although we are equally fragile and easily crushed, Ephesians 5:14 outlines for us what can happen when Christ shines through his people, as they carry his light. The sleepy are roused. The dead are raised. Men and women move out of their darkness into God's marvellous light and become alive to God for the very first time. The inescapable logic of this passage is the sheer inconsistency of being linked up with darkness, while all the while claiming to be in the light. We must be what we are – light in the Lord. If we don't live that way, our profession is worthless. It is the gracious work of the Spirit in our lives not only to show us the pathway, but to enable and empower us to walk it, in practical down-to-earth holiness. He wants to make us more and more like the Lord Jesus.

The Spirit of Wisdom

WALKING IN WISDOM (VV. 15-17)

Once again, the thrust of the teaching here is the exhortation to become, in reality, all that we are, in potential. Evil is not only fruitless; it is also foolish. Christians are to be wise. Living as light should lead to walking in wisdom, but it will not happen automatically. Verse 15 stresses that we have to take care. We are to be "watchful on every side". This means that we need to check up on ourselves and exercise strict self-discipline. A walk is made up of numberless steps, each one small enough in itself, but each counting vitally towards the ultimate destination. As Christians we must literally watch our step!

The unwise go along the line of least resistance, drifting with the crowd, doing the things that everybody does, without thinking through their outcome. The wise, on the other hand, are alert to living in Christ's light, hearing and obeying what Jesus teaches. Their goals are settled and their priorities are clear. The wise Christian will therefore work hard at understanding and applying the Bible's teaching to every aspect of daily life. Only that sort of consistent effort will develop the wisdom by which to live a life of Christian reality, in the midst of a hostile world.

Paul's realism is seen in his reminder that the days are evil. Whether we live in the first or the twenty-first century, we live in an enemy-occupied world. That need not daunt us, but it should serve to discipline and direct us. Time is short and every day counts. Indeed, time is the only one of God's precious gifts that is constantly decreasing, so, wise Christians "redeem" it. The verb means literally to grasp every opportunity to buy up a scarce commodity and make a profit on it, to snap up the bargain. You could use it of the crowds queuing outside a store before the seasonal sale begins. They want to make the best use of their resources. Similarly, the Spirit's work in our lives is to make us astute spiritual investors, but that will not just happen. It requires thoughtful study of scripture, believing prayer and enriching fellowship. They all take time, so Paul's message is,

"Don't waste it; invest it". You can re-utilise almost any kind of waste except waste of time. Every day needs to be used so as to produce the maximum dividend for the kingdom (v. 17).

If that is to happen, then we need to understand what the Lord's path is for us each day, and determine to follow it. Many of us Christians are rather like the old sailor in one of A.A. Milne's poems. He had so many things that he wanted to do "that whenever he thought it was time to begin, he couldn't because of the state he was in." God does not expect us to do everything. He has no desire for his people to become neurotic. To see a need does not in itself constitute a call to meet it. Otherwise, we would all be constantly in transit between needs, hopelessly over-stretched and achieving nothing of lasting value. Even the Lord Jesus did not meet every need. Clearly, there were many sick people in Galilee who were left untreated and unhealed, because he had a greater priority (Luke 4:42-44). But this did not make Jesus restless or frantic. His primary task was to proclaim the good news of the kingdom. So, at the end of his earthly life, just as he was about to return to his heavenly Father, he was able to begin his high-priestly prayer with the affirmation, "I have brought you glory on earth by completing the work you gave me to do." (John 17:4) That was all; but it was everything that mattered. He had not done everything he might have done, because of the finite limitations inherent in his incarnation; but he had done his thing – the task the Father had given him to fulfil. In the same way, we must focus on the Lord's will for our lives today, and then do it with all our might.

There is, however, another perspective on time which Paul is equally keen to inculcate in his readers. It is the contrast between time and eternity, our life in this world and the life of the world to come. Simply to realise that time is a quickly-spent commodity, of finite duration, might lead to a round of frenetic activity to fill our lives to the maximum with the widest possible range of experience. It is what our culture admires as "living life to the full". But while the Christian wants every moment of every day to count for God, there is also the recognition that time belongs to a fallen creation which, because of its evil, is coming to an end. The day will come when God will step on to the stage of human history and bring it to a conclusion. "The world and its desires pass away, but the man who does the will of God lives for ever" (1 John 2:17). The wise Christian, therefore, lives in this world of time, in the light of eternity. Our perspective is to be dictated by God's eternal plan, not by our own short-term goals. This world's agenda has no ultimate significance in God's everlasting kingdom, since it is, at root, a rebellion against his revealed will. But all that we do in this world to serve the king of heaven in the accomplishment of his purposes, in time and space, in human history, will certainly have eternal value, even to a cup of cold water given to the least of Christ's disciples (Matt. 10:42).

The essence of wisdom is to walk in God's will, according to his Word. The Bible provides the principles to govern every step of our walk. We need not only to know them, but to live by them. The Spirit inspired the Word so that we might each have a personal check-list of God's priorities against which we can judge our own. Most of us need to make a regular assessment of our weekly time-table, so that we sort out the important from the urgent and take action where it is needed. Nothing must be allowed to deflect us from doing God's will. But how is that to happen, in practice? The next few verses are crucial to our understanding.

BEING FILLED WITH THE SPIRIT (vv. 18-20)

Verse 18 will repay very careful study, because if we can understand it properly it can help us greatly in our living the Christian life. "Drunk" is the English translation of a Greek word used more widely to mean soaking something, the liquid permeating what is immersed in it and taking over every part. So Paul warns his readers against being soaked with wine, because that will lead to debauchery. The literal meaning is a life of waste, total futility and emptiness, which is the exact opposite of the wise, spiritual investment of life we have just been looking at. Instead, he exhorts them to be continually being filled with the Holy Spirit. But why should the apostle contrast the two conditions in this way?

Do you remember how on the Day of Pentecost when the Spirit's coming was made manifest, some of the crowd in Jerusalem assumed that the apostles must be drunk? The similarity between the two states seems to be that in both cases there is a total control being exercised over the human personality. While the one leads to worthlessness, the other leads to fulfilment. This verse clearly teaches that drunkenness is a sin, in which Christians are not to indulge. When we have found true reality in our relationship with Christ, we do not need alcoholic substitutes. The Christian knows a better way of being lifted above the pressures of life, a better way of overcoming social self-consciousness and feeling at ease with others than by resorting to drink. But the main point of the verse is to illustrate from that negative example the positive content of the command to be filled with the Spirit.

So what does it mean to be "filled with the Spirit" (v. 18)? Interestingly, the New English Bible translates the verse, "Let the Holy Spirit fill you". The fact that the verb is a present imperative indicates not so much an experience as a life-style. The emphasis in the original text is not on crisis so much as continuity. Clearly, Paul does not see what he is advocating as an unusual experience for a spiritual elite, but the norm for every Christian. Indeed, when we reflect on it, the fact becomes obvious that there is no way that we can even begin to live the Christian life at all unless we do so in the power of the Holy Spirit. He is the energy, the dynamic. Every Christian needs the indwelling life of the Spirit to provide that resource, so this cannot be a secret blessing for a chosen few.

Nor is Paul teaching that there is a "second" blessing, following conversion, needed to make us holy, or to put us in a different league of spirituality, beyond the ordinary struggles and problems which all Christians experience in a fallen world. To know the filling of the Spirit is to be experiencing the inflow of the life of God into every part of my life, so that every area of my being is permeated and controlled by him. It is to be a continuing experience like a spring of water perpetually bringing refreshment, cleansing and life to the land through which it flows. Jesus said, "Whoever drinks the water I give him will never thirst. Indeed, the water I give him will become in him a spring of water welling up to eternal life" (John 4:14). And again, "Whoever believes in me, as the Scripture has said, streams of living water will flow from within him. By this he meant the Spirit...." (John 7:38-39). The Biblical picture of fullness is not that I come to a great, climactic experience in which the little cup of my life is filled and then I have to carry it very carefully so that none of it spills out and I do not "lose the blessing". The reality is more like that cup being placed under a continually running tap (or perhaps a better example would be the Niagara Falls!), so that the water constantly flows in and out of it. The cup remains full and yet it overflows the water all around it. Only this picture can begin to do justice to the energy and power of the Holy Spirit. The Spirit's fulness is not a fragile, emotional high that makes me super-spiritual, but a sane, joyous and continuous dependence on the Lord, that makes for a sound mind, and a heart at leisure from itself. We shall see that spelt out in the next chapter, when we come to examine freedom and fulfilment of the Spirit's work, which is the evidence of God's grace in our characters and behaviour.

But the question which naturally arises is that if all this is true, what are we to make of the crisis experiences which many of us have had in our Christian lives? On careful examination, we find that there is usually a common denominator in them all. They are concerned with the removal of many different barriers and blockages, erected by our disobedience, which would otherwise hinder the flow of God's life into every part of our beings. Being filled with the Spirit cannot mean that somehow we get more of the Holy Spirit. Because he is a divine person, he is indivisible. You cannot have half the Spirit within you any more than you could welcome half of your friend to your home. Either they are with you in your home, or they are not! But are they welcome in every room of your home? We have established from the New Testament that every Christian has the Holy Spirit. The question of fulness is therefore a question of whether the Holy Spirit has full, unhindered access to every part and dimension of our lives.

Think of the illustration of a river estuary, with the tide flowing in. The water will gradually seep into and penetrate every area, unless there is a dam or some kind of blockage. If that is so, then the estuary is not filled in that area. Similarly, in our lives, God may reveal to us some particular area where we've held out against Him, and decided to go it alone, in rebellion and disobedience, so that in that part of our lives the whole of our spiritual experience is emptied and dried out. The remedy is to let the Holy Spirit fill you. Let him flow into every area of your being. Only he can be the energy and power which we need in order to live a truly Christian life. We do not simply need to know the Word; we also need the enabling of the Holy Spirit to empower us to obey that Word. Growing strong and maturing as a Christian is not just a matter of Bible study, but of Bible obedience; not just high ideals, or even dogged self-discipline, but God's power.

What will be the result? Verses 19-20 present us with a string of present participles, in Greek, which all depend on the "being filled". The outcome is seen in speaking, singing, proclaiming and giving thanks. They are all products of life and exhilaration. The life which the Spirit brings is expressed in joy. There is something spiritually wrong with a Christian, or a congregation, that does not want to sing God's praise. We must not be content with a joy so deep that it never surfaces! It must first be in the heart, but it also needs to be on the lips, and shared in the fellowship. A spirit-filled believer is above all thankful, gratefully recognising the Father's sovereignty and the Saviour's sufficiency, through the Holy Spirit's ministry. The more we are filled with his life, the more we shall live in the light and walk in his wisdom. Surely that is something to be thankful about, to set our hearts singing.

11.

THE SPIRIT OF PEACE

ROMANS 8:1-17

Therefore, there is now no condemnation for those
who are in Christ Jesus, because through Christ Jesus
the law of the Spirit of life set me free from the law
of sin and death. For what the law was powerless to
do in that it was weakened by the sinful nature, God
did by sending his own Son in the likeness of sinful
man to be a sin offering. And so he condemned sin in
sinful man, in order that the righteous requirements
of the law might be fully met in us, who do not live
according to the sinful nature but according to the
Spirit. Those who live according to the sinful nature
have their minds set on what that nature desires; but
those who live in accordance with the Spirit have
their minds set on what the Spirit desires. The mind
of sinful man is death, but the mind controlled by
the Spirit is life and peace; the sinful mind is hostile
to God. It does not submit to God's law, nor can it
do so. Those controlled by the sinful nature cannot
please God. You, however, are controlled not by
the sinful nature but by the Spirit, if the Spirit of

God lives in you. And if anyone does not have the Spirit of Christ, he does not belong to Christ. But if Christ is in you, your body is dead because of sin, yet your spirit is alive because of righteousness. And if the Spirit of him who raised Jesus from the dead is living in you, he who raised Christ from the dead will also give life to your mortal bodies through his Spirit, who lives in you. Therefore, brothers, we have an obligation – but it is not to the sinful nature, to live according to it. For if you live according to the sinful nature, you will die; but if by the Spirit you put to death the misdeeds of the body, you will live, because those who are led by the Spirit of God are sons of God. For you did not receive a spirit that makes you a slave again to fear, but you received the Spirit of sonship. And by him we cry, "Abba, Father." The Spirit himself testifies with our spirit that we are God's children. Now if we are children, then we are heirs – heirs of God and co-heirs with Christ, if indeed we share in his sufferings in order that we may also share in his glory. (Rom. 8:1-17)

There are some passages of Scripture which stand out like majestic mountain ranges, overwhelming in their grandeur and magnificence. The more you explore them, the more there is to explore. They speak through the different "weathers" of life, with a clarity and relevance, a beauty and strength, that has us coming back again and again to their certainties.

Chapters 5 to 8 of Paul's magisterial letter to the Romans is one such range, which exercises its magnetic pull on Bible-believing Christians, all around the world and in all the variety of life's circumstances. In his masterly expositions of these chapters, first given at Keswick, and then expanded into the book *Men Made New*, John Stott highlights the freedoms which become ours when we believe in Christ. The Christian is set free from the wrath of God (chapter 5), from the power of sin (chapter 6), from the impossible burden of the law (chapter 7) and even from death itself (chapter 8). Just as those four hostile powers, which spoil and destroy human life, are inseparably bound up together, so also God's victory is demonstrated and accomplished in the one great reality of our eternal salvation, through the death and resurrection of Jesus Christ. It is through this great objective fact of Christ's death for the ungodly that we are freely forgiven. United with Christ in his death, we have died to sin. United with him in his resurrection, we walk in newness of life. And yet...

Those great certainties of chapters 5 and 6 cannot obscure the reality of the struggle with sin which Paul so graphically documents in chapter 7, and which every Christian knows through daily, personal experience. "So I find this law at work: when I want to do good, evil is right there with me. For in my inner being I delight in God's law; but I see another law at work in the members of my body, waging war against the law of my mind and making me a prisoner of the law of sin at work within my members. What a wretched man I am! Who will rescue me from the body of death? Thanks be to God – through Jesus Christ our Lord! So, then, I myself in my mind am a slave to God's law, but in the sinful nature a slave to the law of sin" (Rom. 7:21-25). That is how Romans 7 ends. It is Paul's present-tense experience. That alone should warn us against an over-easy and misleading exegesis of the material, which implies that there is some way in which we can move, once and for all, out of Romans 7 and into the triumph of Romans 8. We do not move out of that tension into undisturbed spiritual peace in this world. That will be the ultimate solution, when the Lord Jesus delivers us from this body of death and we are fully united with him, in glory. But the peace which the Spirit gives here and now is the ability to live fruitfully in the midst of the tension between what is ours already and what is not yet ours.

In fact, that is the theme which runs all the way through these chapters in Romans. It is only by the Spirit's work, within the Christian, that we can faithfully live here in this world, as citizens of heaven. In a famous phrase from the Reformation, the Christian experience here is described as *simul justus et peccator* – at the same time justified and a sinner. That is the tension Paul explores in these chapters. What is our freedom in Christ, if we are still subject to sin's presence? None of us can deny that to be a reality in our lives; we are not yet made perfect. In chapter 8, Paul faces the tension in terms that we feel deeply in every bereavement, at every funeral service. How do believers, who are alive in Christ for ever, cope with the present realities of suffering and death? They are different reflections of this same issue, which occupies so much of our earthly experience – the tension between what is ours already, in Christ, and what cannot be ours until heaven.

One temptingly easy way to try to resolve the tension is to deny the "now" experience entirely. Historically, this has always been the attraction of perfectionism. It actually involves moving the goal posts, in the sense that sin has to be redefined, so as to exclude our present failings and weaknesses. The parallel in the physical realm would be to claim that some one has been healed from a disease, although they are still suffering the symptoms. If we lower our standard of holiness to what we are capable of achieving, then it is possible to claim to have arrived.

The other, more popular, way of resolving the tension is to pull the "not-yet" into the present, making its enjoyment dependent only on the exercise of our faith. The appeal is seen in the "prosperity gospel" where wealth, health and wisdom are available here and now, if only faith is strong enough to identify and claim the promises. Like the famous credit-card advertisement, this teaching "takes the waiting out of wanting". It seems at root to be a Christianised version of the current secular culture, which is itself increasingly attracted to the promises of heaven on earth held out by scientific and technological advances and the growth of material prosperity.

Of course, I am not wanting to deny the great blessings of the gospel that we do enjoy already, nor am I suggesting that we could not know far more of the grace of God and the power of the Spirit than we have yet experienced, here in this world. Isaac Watts was right when he wrote, "The men of grace have found glory begun below". But the point is that it is only a beginning. We have "the first-fruits of the Spirit", which is why we "groan inwardly as we wait eagerly for our adoption as sons, the redemption of our bodies" (Rom. 8:23). To deny that as a real and lasting tension of our human condition, as redeemed sinners, is to end up living in unreality. It is the spiritual equivalent of the drop-out culture, which is of no earthly use to anyone.

The point is made very explicitly by Paul at the beginning of this great section in Romans 5, where he starts to explore the outcome of what it means to be justified freely by God's grace, through faith in Christ. He has already established justification as the universal need (1:18-3:20) and described the process by which it happens (3:21-4:25). In Romans 5:1, Paul affirms that "Since we have been justified through faith, we have peace with God through our Lord Jesus Christ." When we talk about peace today, we instinctively think about subjective feelings, or emotions. But we cannot stress too much that what Paul is talking about is the objective reality of being at peace with God, instead of being at war. "We were reconciled to God through the death of his Son" he reminds us in 5:10. It has happened! God has conferred to us the state of being in the right with him and brought us into a family relationship, as adopted children. This is the "grace in which we now stand", by faith (5:2).

Significantly, Paul continues, "and we rejoice...". That too is part of our present experience. But our present joy is generated by what we do not yet see. "We rejoice in the hope of the glory of God" (5:2b). That far horizon of what we shall one day be, when we see him face to face, dominates our thinking so much that we are able to rejoice in the midst of our present tensions and difficulties. Paul goes on, "Not only so, but we also rejoice in our sufferings..." (5:3) and the subsequent clauses show how they produce perseverance, character and a hope that will never be disappointed. All this is ours because "God has poured out his love into our hearts by the Holy Spirit, whom he has given us" (5:5).

The work of the Spirit of peace, then, is to assure believers of God's love, by making their justification a living reality at the very heart and core of their Christian discipleship. He is not given to "air-lift" us out of the stresses and pressures of living as forgiven sinners with our fallen, human natures, in a fallen world. The mark of the Spirit's work is that we rejoice in God's justifying grace and love in the midst of it all and learn to live these days on earth in the light of that great day, as citizens of heaven. With these principles established, we can now turn back to Romans 8 and understand its teaching, in context, more clearly and powerfully.

THE SPIRIT TEACHES US WHAT HAS HAPPENED (VV. 1-8)

It is not surprising to see that the chapter begins by reaffirming and expounding the blessings of justification by faith. To be in Christ means to be declared "not guilty" by God, just as if I had never sinned. That is so amazing that it takes most of us a very long time to grasp its implications. Our judicial standing is that in Christ we are acquitted – there is no condemnation. Verse 2 explores the mechanism. The "law of sin and death" is the principle by which my sinful human nature expresses its rebellion against God and therefore places itself under the righteous sentence of his wrath. That "law" imprisons every sinner, just as surely as the law of gravity binds us to the earth. But God's gift in salvation of the Holy Spirit, the giver of life, becomes the new dominating principle in the life of the justified sinner. His control sets me free from the dominance of sin, as promised in Romans 6:14. It is important to note that the phrase "through Christ Jesus" points to the centrality of the work of the Saviour on the cross, as the pre-requisite and basis for the Spirit's liberating work in my life. There can be neither peace nor power without pardon.

As we have already seen, this is the radical change which has occurred to make a sinner into a Christian. The evidence is seen in the struggle that has now commenced. Our freedom has not yet brought the full fruits of victory, but it does give us the liberty to continue the conflict. When we say that the gospel liberates us from sin, we do not mean that we are sinlessly perfect but that we are free from sin's tyranny. It is no longer "calling the shots". Similarly, when we say we have been liberated from death, through the eternal life which is already ours, in Christ, we do not mean that we shall not experience death, or sickness, pain and suffering, but that death no longer has the last word. We know the one because we experience the other.

The fact that all this depends entirely upon the initiative which God has taken, in Christ, is the emphasis in verse 3. God has done what the law could never do. Because of our sinful nature (the flesh) we cannot keep God's holy law. We are justly condemned and in bondage. What the law could not do was to give life. Actually, it kills. "For if a law had been given that could impart life, then righteousness would certainly have come by the law. But the Scripture declares that the whole world is a prisoner of sin, so that what was promised, being given through faith in Jesus Christ, might be given to those who believe" (Gal. 3:21-22). By this intervention of God, all that has been changed.

The normal human story is that sin condemns man. But, as a sinless man, the Lord Jesus has condemned sin, and done this in the very human nature in which he was exposed to all the rigours of the fiercest temptations. His sinless life prepared the way for his atoning death. God condemned our sin, in the sinless person of the Lord Jesus, as He carried all our guilt in His own body, on the cross. That is what happened in history, but verse 4 tells us what has happened in our experience, as a result.

This is a verse that has often been misunderstood. Does it say that Christians have been so changed that we can fulfil all the requirements of the law, by our works of righteousness? It would mean that while we recognise that at one time we could never have lived up to the standards of God's righteousness, as revealed in the law, now we have received the Spirit and so we can do it. If we think that is what Paul is teaching we shall certainly not experience much peace, because we do not and cannot achieve that standard, even as believers. The tragedy is that it can easily set us off on a false quest. Many Christians have lost their joy and peace because they know they are not perfect and so have mistakenly labelled themselves "carnal". They begin an endless round of seeking a crisis experience that will change it all, at a stroke. But that is not what the apostle is actually teaching here.

It is not our holiness that justifies us, but God's grace. We are not made right with God on the grounds of what we will become. That would be to make the law the goal and to reduce the gospel to being the means by which we hope to reach it. The Holy Spirit is then reduced to supplying the little bit extra we need to make it to God. No; that is to stand the New Testament on its head! The law can only condemn. We are declared righteous solely because of Jesus, because we are "in him". He is the righteousness of God, in himself. The great change that happens, as a result of regeneration, is that we do not live according to the flesh, but according to the Spirit.

It follows, therefore, that verses 5-8 are not about the contrast between carnal and spiritual Christians, but about the difference between being a Christian and not yet being a Christian. From these verses, we can work out what has happened in our Christian experience since the Holy Spirit came to take up residence in our lives. Life before conversion is described as being set on what the sinful nature desires (v. 5), destined for death (v. 6), hostile to God (v. 7) and controlled by the flesh (v. 8). All this changes fundamentally through the new birth. God declares us forgiven and free, so that nothing can destroy that work of Christ on our behalf. The focus of peace and security is not in our works, but in Christ, our righteousness.

THE SPIRIT TEACHES US WHO WE ARE (vv. 9-11)

Here is the great distinguishing mark of all true Christians – "the Holy Spirit of God lives in you" (v. 9). Paul expresses the same fact in verse 10 as "Christ is in you". We must not be confused by the trinitarian language here, as Paul refers to "the Spirit of God" and "the Spirit of Christ". Since God is a unity, they are one and the same. You cannot be a Christian without having the Holy Spirit. Nowhere in the New Testament are we taught that the Holy Spirit is to be received in a separate second experience, following conversion – quite the opposite, in fact. If you are in Christ, by faith, then his Spirit is within you, which means that you are not controlled by the sinful nature, the flesh (v. 9). We are to see ourselves as God sees us. We belong to Christ. His Spirit is within us. We need to know who we are!

In order to help us do that, two significant consequences are explained in verses 10-11. One is present, the other is future. In the present, we live with the fact that our bodies are mortal and they are going to die. That is the consequence of the fall, in the coming of sin as the universal infection of the human race. "The wages of sin is death" (6:23). Spiritually, however, we are alive because of Christ's righteousness, and having been made right with God through his Son, we share in his eternal life by his Spirit. That leads to the future consequence in verse 11.

Through the Spirit, we are set free from death's tyranny, in the sense that the experience we call death becomes the "gate to life immortal". Moreover, on the last day, we shall be given new resurrection bodies, made like Christ's glorious body, in which we shall live with him for ever. We do have Christ in our hearts now, and with him, the hope of the glory that lies ahead. This is the healthy fresh air of Christian realism. We are eternally and spiritually alive in Christ, but in earthly bodies that will die one day, if Christ does not return first. That is the inevitable consequence of the fall, and while the grace of God transcends it, he does not undo it. Our peace comes in letting the Holy Spirit teach us what we are – sinful, mortal, fragile human beings, but by God's grace we are also justified, redeemed and bound for glory!

THE SPIRIT TEACHES US HOW TO LIVE (VV. 12-17)

These wonderful verses teach us how practically to cope with the tension between the flesh and the Spirit in our present experience. They illustrate how the Spirit of peace leads and enables us in living the normal Christian life. Perhaps we can best focus this teaching by noting the three ingredients of Christian living which are each related to that little phrase "by the Spirit", as it occurs in verses 13, 14, and 15. Verse 12 makes it very clear that the Holy Spirit is given to us to enable us to fulfil our obligation, as born again Christians, to live a Christ-like life. We are not to live according to the flesh, which leads to spiritual death. Therefore, it is by the Spirit that we are to put to death the misdeeds of the body (v. 13).

The verse contains that characteristic New Testament blend, or balance, of God's initiative and provision with our responsibility to respond. It stresses our response to his ability. All through the Bible, command and promise are woven together, as we are called to trust and obey. There is a strong Biblical logic operating here. Because in fact we are no longer controlled by the sinful nature, we are not to live as though we were. Our obligation is not to live a life of asceticism for its own sake, much less a life of spiritual masochism, which believes the more it hurts the more good it must be doing, but to see to it that we are not governed by the appetites and desires of the flesh. They will only nurture the self-centredness which expresses itself in pride and developing independence from God.

We are debtors, and we must never forget it. Rightly to understand what it means to be justified is in itself a great motivation to holy living. There are practical implications. It means calling sin by its real name and recognising it for what it is. It involves an up-to-date repentance, asking God's forgiveness for all known sins in our lives, and being prepared to cut them out. We cannot dally with them and indulge them; rather, we need to overcome and get rid of them, by the power of the Holy Spirit, as we open up those specific areas of our lives to him, asking for his cleansing and a new filling of his grace and power.

Secondly, we learn that it is by the Spirit that God's children are led (v. 14). That does not imply unhindered progress, but it does mean that our lives are to be set in the direction of doing God's will and going God's way. God is not the Father of every human being, though he is the creator of all. The status of children is limited to those who are being led by the Spirit, enabled by him to walk the pathway of obedience to the Father's will. The Spirit's leading, then, in this context, is not so much detailed guidance regarding the circumstances of life, or the choices we might make, but more the inner prompting and enabling to put to death the misdeeds, or scheming intrigues (literally) of the sinful flesh, that is always wanting to assert itself. It is important to recognise how little, when we refer to the Lord leading us today, we mean into holiness, and how often the phrase is used merely to justify a personal circumstantial decision. While I would not want to deny that God can and does give us wisdom to choose well in the details of our lives, it is significant that the Bible's emphasis is clearly on the pathway of godliness.

Lastly, in verse 15, we learn that it is by the Spirit that we call God "Father". Praise God that we do not live in bondage to fear! That is the essence of all non-Christian religion, which binds men and women to follow its rituals and teaching, in order to escape their fear of punishment and retribution for not doing so. The good news of the Christian faith is that our God makes us his sons and daughters out of his own love and grace. He sends his Spirit into our innermost beings, so that as we daily turn from sin and daily fight the battle with the flesh, we can cry out to him as "Father" – "Abba", which is the Aramaic family word of intimacy and love. This was the very word the Lord Jesus used in his own praying. So, the work of the Spirit of peace within us is to assure us, in the midst of all life's battles, that this relationship of a child to a loving father is the greatest reality of our lives, unshakable and eternal (v. 16). What an amazing privilege and blessing that is! We do not have to be weighed down by the unanswerable questions of those who are merely religious. Have I done enough? Did I get it right? Shall I be accepted? The Holy Spirit does not take us that route. He teaches us that we are accepted, in the beloved Son, and enables us to experience a deep, personal, love-relationship of trust and confidence in our "Abba". He brings us into the family and unites us together as brothers and sisters. He gives us that assurance, which we could never generate within ourselves, that we really are God's children (v. 16).

Is the evidence of that assurance perfect bliss, or unalloyed happiness? Are we guaranteed always to be healthy, wealthy and wise? Not according to verse 17! We are co-heirs with a Saviour who walked the path of suffering to bring many children home to glory, and we are called to follow in his footsteps. When these Roman Christians were later called upon to face the wild beasts in the arena, or to burn as torches to light the Emperor Nero's gardens, it was not a sign that their faith was deficient. Their God had not given them up and refused to accept them any longer as his children. It was not even a sign that circumstantially everything had gone wrong. Their hearts were comforted in the knowledge that those who share in his sufferings will also share in his glory. They were not called upon to believe that God would reverse all the consequences of the fall here and now, or to imagine that sufficient faith could produce heaven on earth. They were conscious of having "better and lasting possessions". They were "longing for a better country

– a heavenly one" (Heb. 10:34, 11:16). They knew what we have largely forgotten, that co-heirs with Christ do suffer, but they also knew that the pathway leads to glory. The Spirit of peace was given not only to teach Christians of all generations these great eternal realities, but also, in the light of them, to enable us all to live normal Christian lives. That is nothing less than supernatural!

12.

THE SPIRIT OF POWER

ROMANS 8:18-39

I consider that our present sufferings are not worth comparing with the glory that will be revealed in us. The creation waits in eager expectation for the sons of God to be revealed. For the creation was subjected to frustration, not by its own choice, but by the will of the one who subjected it, in hope that the creation itself will be liberated from its bondage to decay and brought into the glorious freedom of the children of God. We know that the whole creation has been groaning as in the pains of childbirth right up to the present time. Not only so, but we ourselves, who have the firstfruits of the Spirit, groan inwardly as we wait eagerly for our adoption as sons, the redemption of our bodies. For in this hope we were saved. But hope that is seen is no hope at all. Who hopes for what he already has? But if we hope for what we do not yet have, we wait for it patiently. In the same way, the Spirit helps us in our weakness. We do not know what we ought to pray for, but the Spirit himself intercedes for us with groans that words cannot express. And he who searches our hearts knows the mind of the Spirit, because the Spirit intercedes for the saints in accordance with God's will.

And we know that in all things God works for the good of those who love him, who have been called according to his purpose. For those God foreknew he also predestined to be conformed to the likeness of his Son, that he might be the firstborn among many brothers. And those he predestined, he also called; those he called, he also justified; those he justified, he also glorified. What, then, shall we say in response to this? If God is for us, who can be against us? He who did not spare his own Son, but gave him up for us all – how will he not also, along with him, graciously give us all things? Who will bring any charge against those whom God has chosen? It is God who justifies. Who is he that condemns? Christ Jesus, who died – more than that, who was raised to life – is at the right hand of God and is also interceding for us. Who shall separate us from the love of Christ? Shall trouble or hardship or persecution or famine or nakedness or danger or sword? As it is written: "For your sake we face death all day long; we are considered as sheep to be slaughtered." No, in all these things we are more than conquerors through him who loved us. For I am convinced that neither death nor life, neither angels nor demons, neither the present nor the future, nor any powers, neither height nor depth, nor anything else in all creation, will be able to separate us from the love of God that is in Christ Jesus our Lord. (Rom. 8:18-39)

We live in a power-hungry world. But much more important than the acquisition of power is its use. Many an individual who has been highly successful in the business of gaining power has proved to be a hollow failure, almost a nonentity, when it came to using the power he had struggled so hard to acquire. In church life we are influenced by the spirit of the age far more than we are prepared to admit. In every generation, one of the key struggles for the people of God is to counteract the pressure of the culture squeezing them into its mould. So, for the last thirty years at least, there has been an increasing emphasis among Christians on the quest for spiritual power. Kilos of books have poured off the presses and endless conferences have been convened on the subject of power in Christian living, in prayer, in evangelism, in healing. Naturally, in all these contexts there has been a great deal of teaching on the Holy Spirit, nearly always in terms of power. Did not Jesus promise "You will receive power when the Holy Spirit comes on you" (Acts 1:8)? In that situation it was power "to be my witnesses". But it is never power for its own sake, in Scripture. The enabling of the Spirit is always for a definite purpose. As we turn to this second half of Romans 8, which as a chapter has so much to say about the ministry of the Holy Spirit, the divine enabler, we need to learn from Scripture what God's purposes are in empowering his people.

POWER TO LIVE IN THE REAL WORLD (vv. 18-27)

What is the picture of life in this present world put before us by the apostle Paul in these verses? Verse 18 speaks of "our present sufferings", and in the last section we saw that this is an inescapable part of what it means to be co-heirs with Christ (v. 17). It has an unavoidable place in our Christian experience in this world. We follow a Saviour whose path led through suffering to glory, a pattern which becomes the norm for his disciples who are called to take up their cross to follow him. So suffering is not some appalling abnormality indicating that God has rejected me, or is no longer loving me. It has to be expected in this world, not only because of the nature of our discipleship, but also because our world is itself "subjected to frustration" (v. 20a).

There is a futility about much of human life and experience which the whole Old Testament book of Ecclesiastes explores in depth. This is the meaninglessness which our contemporary culture feels so acutely, because of the "bondage to decay" in which it exists (v. 21). The continuous cycle of birth, growth, maturity, death and decomposition is representative of a universe that is deteriorating, running down. That is why we find so many people asking, "What's the point?" So much of the artistic creativity of our times has been occupied with this challenge of coming to terms with the ultimate reality of death. Writers have railed against it and sought to preserve in their work something of the immortality for which they instinctively felt themselves to have been born. But Shakespeare surely made the point most poignantly centuries ago when he wrote, "Gilded boys and girls all must, like chimney sweepers, come to dust." We belong to a creation that is groaning (v. 22). There is a longing for release, for something better.

At this point we often think and speak of the gospel and the power of the life-giving Holy Spirit as the answer to the human dilemma – and we are right. But we expect the answer to be applied in the wrong way. We imagine that God's power should be a sort of spiritual rocket, to lift us up, like a space shuttle, beyond the gravitational pull of this world, into an entirely different orbit. Just as many non-Christians look for release in the ultimate experience, so many Christians are similarly hoping to find some way of living beyond the "present sufferings" altogether. They really want to be living in another world. But that's not what the Bible is telling us about life on planet earth, here in Romans 8. Look at what Paul says about Christians in verse 23. We groan too! Is that not true?

Even though we are already God's children by his grace (v. 14), we do not yet have our redeemed bodies. There is a sense in which we are saved, and yet not saved. Remember the message of verse 10 that "your body is dead because of sin, yet your Spirit is alive because of righteousness". Physically, we are fragile and easily broken. We soon grow weary and discouraged. We become ill; we suffer pain; we die. It is no part of powerful Christian living to attempt to deny those facts. Spiritually too, we wrestle with our fallen human nature and our wretched propensity to sin. Christians groan because of what verse 26 describes as "our weakness" linked particularly in that context to our ignorance in prayer. We do not know how to pray because we do not know what is best for us. We may begin well but quickly give up; we are so easily distracted. We are infants in God's school of prayer, because we have so little grasp on what the will of God really is. Paul, the realist, wants us to understand what life is like in this fallen world. If we put his vocabulary together, we find he is speaking about suffering, frustration, decay, groaning and weakness.

Anyone might be excused for writing off that list as a depressing and demotivating catalogue, if that is all there is to be said. Thank God there is much more to be understood; but unless we hear and receive the negative side first, we shall condemn ourselves to live in a world of make-believe, a fantasy-land of pseudo-piety. However, throughout these verses, another strand has been running parallel, and this must now be our focus. Verses 18-19 may speak about our present suffering, but in total contrast they also direct us to the future glory which is beyond all comparison. Similarly, the created world that is subject to frustration and decay in verse 19 is also seen to be waiting in eager expectation, on tip-toe, as it were, for the sons of God to be revealed. Through man's sin, death has come to dominate this world. Even the earth itself was cursed because of man's fall (Gen. 3:17). But although the creation has been made subject to corruption because of man's sin, it is not without hope. Another man has appeared, Jesus Christ – the "proper" man, chosen by God, one in whom the claims of divine righteousness have been perfectly fulfilled. Because the seed of the woman has crushed the serpent's head, there is the promise of new heavens and a new earth, the home of righteousness.

That is why the present groaning (v. 22) is not purposeless. The pains of childbirth are bringing something new and wonderful into the world. So creation's groaning is part of the process by which the new order, the new creation, is brought to birth. And it is that order which will bring with it the freedom of glory. That is when the rocket motor really will boost us into a new orbit; not now. Present Christian experience combines inward groaning with eager waiting (v. 23). We have the first fruits of the Spirit, as he lives within us, but we do not yet have the full harvest.

All this means that the predominant characteristic of the Christian's life in the present world is hope. When verse 24 tells us that "in this hope we were saved", it is stating that this has been so from the very start of our Christian experience, and will be, right the way through, until hope vanishes into sight. The aorist tense ("we were saved") indicates a fixed certainty, which is designed to increase our confidence. On the basis of the first fruits of the Spirit, which we are already enjoying, we can have a sure and certain hope for what is not yet ours. It is the Spirit's work within us to underline and assure us of our guaranteed inheritance, by the grace of God. This is the foretaste of that full salvation for which we long, in terms of our redeemed bodies and the glory of God's presence. But, at present, the power of the Spirit is demonstrated in our waiting eagerly (v. 23) and patiently (v. 25). He is the one who takes our earth-bound longings and fixes them above. Our natural goals are happiness and comfort; his goals for us are holiness and heaven.

In this half-way situation, it is the indwelling Holy Spirit who teaches us to pray. When we experience "those agonising longings which never find words" (J.B. Phillips) we can have confidence that the Spirit is interceding for us. God knows our thoughts; he hears our sighs and searches our hearts. The power of the Spirit is seen in the fact that he does know God's perfect will and prays for it to be outworked in us. There is a certain relief in those words of verse 26, "we do not know what we ought to pray for". It might not be a confession we would eagerly make, but it is the truth of the matter. It is an expression, as well as a symptom, of our weakness. We do cry "Abba" and we do know what it is to turn to God in believing prayer, but few of us do it nearly consistently enough. Once again, however, we are being taught that in our prayer life, as in every other aspect of our discipleship, we are entirely dependent on the ministry of the Spirit. He intercedes for us. It is not the techniques which matter – the vocabulary or formulae – but the sincere expression of our total dependence on God. If you analyse it, you will find that to be the difference between the prophets of Baal and Elijah in the great prayer contest on Mount Carmel (1 Kings 18). The one is all about performance; the other about dependence. That is why inarticulate groaning can be effective praying, for even the Spirit groans (v. 26), as well as creation (v. 22) and believers (v. 23). As a result, our "Abba", who knows our hearts and the unspoken desire of his Spirit within us, works out his purpose of grace within our lives, by bringing every situation of our need in line with his will.

POWER TO LIVE IN THE DIVINE CERTAINTIES (VV. 28-39)

These are very familiar and treasured verses to many of us and the great danger is that we have become over familiar with what they are saying. Let us recognise that verse 28 is not just a wonderful promise to claim in times of difficulty. It is a bedrock foundation on which the whole of our Christian experience must be built. What is the will of God for which the Spirit is interceding on behalf of the saints, in verse 27? It is the good of those who love him. There is some discussion as to whether the subject of the verb "work" in verse 28 is "all things" (as in the AV and RV) or "God" (as in the NIV and most modern translations). Personally, I favour the latter since it makes the total control of the sovereign Lord in every circumstance of life transparently clear, which must be the main meaning of the verse. Even the things which seem most against us, most likely to hurt or harm us, are actually being woven together to work for our truest and ultimate good. They are all permitted and used by our heavenly Father, not at all with the aim of our present comfort, but for our eternal benefit. They cannot therefore harm those who really love God.

It is so important to grasp this, because God wants us to have firm convictions about the direction he is taking in our lives, in order to fulfil his plan of salvation in us and through us. We can and must trust God, even when "all things" seem to be most hopeless. For the same Spirit who intercedes for us is equally active in all the circumstances of our lives. This is the outcome of Christ's justifying work on the cross. He has conquered all the hostile powers that were ranged against us, as these chapters have constantly affirmed, and they are powerless before him. It is the victorious, risen and ascended Christ who proclaims, "Do not be afraid. I am the First and the Last. I am the Living One; I was dead and behold I am alive for ever and ever! And I hold the keys of death and Hades" (what lies beyond) – Rev. 1:17-18. So we do not need to fear the enemy. He does not win any rounds. He is totally subject to the authority of his creator and subduer, whose sovereign will cannot be undermined, either by our inadequacy or our failures.

Whatever the mysteries of God's foreknowledge and predestination, the purpose of it all is made crystal clear in verse 29. He has chosen us to be holy, to become more and more like the Lord Jesus. Just as at the beginning God created man by a sovereign act, in his own image, so by a parallel sovereign act, he has predestined all his people to be conformed to the image of his Son. In order to accomplish this, he has called us to himself and justified us freely by his grace, so that we are accepted, in Christ, as God's dearly loved children. It is therefore equally certain that we shall be glorified. That is why the past tense is used in verse 30, since in God's eyes it has already happened. It is the inevitable conclusion of the whole process. It is that certain! The Spirit works powerfully within us now, to stimulate our desires to become more like the Lord Jesus. He sustains us as we long and wait for the future glory, when we shall see him as he is and be completely transformed into his likeness.

There are times when the hope of heaven can appear to be so remote as to seem almost escapist, in the midst of all our current difficulties and challenges, here on earth. We are all too easily conditioned by the world's derogatory assessment of the likelihood of heaven as "pie in the sky when you die", so that our expectation is weakened, our gratitude dulled and our motivation compromised. Of course, we still hold on to heaven as a doctrinal belief, but it has little real impact on the way we live our daily lives. Even at our best, we tend to measure the eternal unseen glories of heaven by the limitations of our earthly experience of salvation, in the present. But instead of using our experience as the measure of all that God has for us, Paul encourages his readers to evaluate their glorious future by the greatest event of human history—the cross of Christ.

If God did not spare his own beloved Son, but gave him up for us all, can there be any limit as to what his grace will bestow on his dearly-loved adopted children (v. 32)? Not only does his death remove the barrier of our sin and turn away God's righteous wrath from us, as guilty sinners, but it also spells his triumph over all the hostile powers ranged against his sovereign rule and the human creation, made in his image. Death is defeated and Satan is conquered in the death of God's Son, as the ensuing resurrection, in all its historical certainty, so convincingly proved and resoundingly proclaimed. It is perhaps because we are still inevitably so earth-bound and so limited in our ability to comprehend heaven that its greatest pictorial description in the whole Bible, in Revelation 21-22, is partly expressed in negative terms. "No more death or mourning or crying or pain, for the old order of things has passed away" (Rev. 21:4). "No sun or moon to shine on it [the heavenly Jerusalem]…no shut gates…nothing impure, shameful or deceitful…no longer any curse…no more night" (Rev. 21:23, 25, 27; 22:3, 5). It is almost as though we cannot begin to understand our future glory until we see it as the polar opposite to everything that hinders and spoils our experience of God's good gift of life, in this fallen creation. I find that much more concrete than the somewhat elusive visual imagery of clouds and harps and angel choirs which sprinkle our conventional imagination of the life of the world to come.

The worship of heaven becomes something far more wonderful and fulfilling than endless singing, when once we restore the concept behind the term to its original Biblical richness. Because "worship" in much popular Christian thinking is limited to the music that fills our church services before the teaching of God's Word (or sometimes even instead of teaching God's Word), our view of heavenly worship is equivalently impoverished. It motivates us to long for heaven as little as does the concept of eternal rest being defined as "doing nothing for ever and ever". On the contrary, New Testament "worship" is the offering of the whole life in loving obedience and joyful service to our Lord Jesus Christ (Rom. 12:1-2), of which corporate singing is just one tiny feature. "Love so amazing, so divine, demands my soul, my life, my all." And if that is true of our worship in this world, with all its frustrations and imperfections, what will it be in the coming heavenly kingdom? It is bound to be immeasurably richer, deeper, more fulfilling and satisfying than anything we have ever experienced on earth.

To be able to serve our risen Lord, in a totally renewed universe, in resurrection bodies like his body of glory, without any of the weaknesses, infirmities, inadequacies and sinfulness of our present existence is the most exciting prospect any human being could anticipate. To see him face to face, to be transformed into his likeness, to love him without variation, to praise him as he truly deserves, to be occupied in the perfect freedom which constitutes his service—these are the future realities to which the Spirit points us and by which he woos us away from living for the trivia of time and sense. We are called to a determined focus on these eternal realities, which really do matter most of all. That is the evidence of the Spirit's power in our lives here and now, for nothing and no one else could begin to produce such a change in our priorities, hopes and goals.

This great chapter ends with the application of these divine certainties to all the challenges and uncertainties of life in this changing world. In five pertinent and penetrating questions, Paul enshrines five majestic, ringing assurances, which nothing can shake. We may face all sorts of enemies – the world, the flesh and the devil; sin and death itself. But none of them is stronger than the God who is for us (v. 31). He could not have proved that more completely than by giving up his only Son for us all, on the cross. Since there is nothing beyond the Lord Jesus that God could give, nothing less will ever be denied to us, his children, provided that, is truly for our eternal good (v. 32). Since God the judge has justified us, no one else can condemn. The Christ, who died for our sins, was raised again for our justification. He has ascended to the Father's right hand in glory, and there he pleads for us as our advocate, our great High Priest (vv. 33-34). Therefore, we can have absolute confidence that nothing ever will, or ever could, be able to separate us from the love of Christ (v. 35). There will be plenty of challenges. But we have seen that they are the norm for Christians living in a fallen and hostile world. We may find that hard to accept in our power-hungry culture, where personal comfort, security and ease are the common goals. But that is precisely why we have the Spirit. His power is seen by Paul not in extricating believers from life's challenges and trials, but in bringing every one of his chosen people to experience Christ's victory in them all.

What then are we to conclude is the mark of the Spirit-filled life in Romans 8? Surely it is the deep-seated convictions of verses 37-39. In spite of all our weakness and failure, in spite of all our suffering and frustration, in spite of the devil and the world, in spite of death itself, the victory is the Lord's! Nothing can separate us from his love now and nothing will keep us from his glory, for ever. When the cross is our focus here and the glory of heaven our certainty hereafter, we are living in the power of the Spirit.